College and the Art of Partying

College and the Art of Partying

Mark R. Dye

Writers Club Press
San Jose New York Lincoln Shanghai

College and the Art of Partying

All Rights Reserved © 2000 by Mark R. Dye

No part of this book may be reproduced or transmitted in any form or by any means, graphic, electronic, or mechanical, including photocopying, recording, taping, or by any information storage retrieval system, without the permission in writing from the publisher.

Writers Club Press
an imprint of iUniverse.com, Inc.

For information address:
iUniverse.com, Inc.
5220 S 16th, Ste. 200
Lincoln, NE 68512
www.iuniverse.com

ISBN: 0-595-12076-8

Printed in the United States of America

Life is not an apology.

—Jack Kerouac

Preface

Technically this is the spot for the preface; mine's more of an apology or a justification or something. This book, as the title suggests, is a simple, descriptive guide to college and partying. It's pretty straightforward. The reader never has to concern him- or herself with getting lost in complicated plot twists and foreshadowing and the like. Any flashbacks encountered are strictly of the unintentional kind. A few remarks should be made regarding style, however.

The first thing the reader will notice about this thing is it describes situations mostly in narrative fashion, which is dead wrong according to most of your present or past college professors. See, these folks have this obsession with writers using lots of direct quotations for the characters. Pick up any old book assigned by a college prof—it'll be heavy with quotation marks. I think the things are designed to get to know the character on a personal level so you weep like a baby when she croaks at the end, 'cause it's like losing your best friend or something. And that's further accomplished through realistic dialog, sometimes with a slangy bent to it for a homesy feel or some crap like that.

But the problem here is none of *my* stuff is made up, like the work of Hemingway and Fitzgerald and all the other bullshitters out there. And even though the events I'm describing occurred recently, given the mad circumstances, who can remember all the he-said she-said crap? Not me at least. For one thing my short and long-term memory is about shot;

generally the music's too loud to hear anything anyway. So you'll find you never really get to know any of the characters too well, except for me. Actually including me. But it's my fuckin' book. Let *them* write one if they feel neglected. Anyway, I *have* made an effort to throw in some character quotes here and there, but it's mainly for aesthetic reasons. One thing's for sure: they make a page *look* damn good. "I think that's how all the nonsense got started in the first place."

A note to female readers: You'll notice a distinct male perspective throughout much of the book. Sorry, but it was impossible to avoid, given the material. May I ask that you tolerantly skim over these parts. The advantage is that for you folks, the thing can be read in one quick toilet sitting.

I'll be honest here. I wasn't my first choice to write this. It's just that discussing college life for the AOPers (I'll tell you later) at Colorado State University is somewhat of a sordid undertaking, and is thus difficult to characterize properly. It's a catch-22 situation. Herein lies the problem: First instinct was to enlist a professional writer who actually knows something about plot construction, character development and theme thickening. Trouble is, these serious sorts generally want no part of a book that regularly mentions vomit and masturbation (in the same sentence). They believe if they contract out for such a book, future book offers will dry up. Why, you ask? Because the writer's present book is no less than a grand advertisement of the artist, fool. It sets the stage for all subsequent books. You think an earnest writer with mouths to feed is gonna sell the farm just so some reader can get his rocks off, get his kicks? You've gotta be nuts. Nine times outta 10 these literary sorts will pour their hearts out for you; just don't expect them to stoop to describing life on the west end of the eleventh floor in Westfall Hall. You'll be messing with their livelihood, buster.

So you're stuck with me. I'll be the first to admit my writing experience is limited, although I do jot letters to my parents pretty often. If anyone's interested, I pulled off a "B" last semester in creative writing.

I'll guarantee the reader one thing though—and this is starting to sound like some sort of campaign—this writer sure ain't thinking no three books ahead like the above clowns. This one alone is more than I can handle. I got characters coming and going—hell if I can keep 'em straight. I had a name conversion chart so no one would sue me, then I think I tossed it with some junk mail, so who knows who's who anymore. I got chicks popping up, screaming, "Lawdy big boy, we're rich! We're rich!!" only to never be heard from again. Characters dropping in and out like lazy flies. Also, you don't need a magnifying glass to see that things don't follow too logically. Like that catch-22 remark mentioned earlier—that makes not a lick of sense. It's not catch-22 at all; it's a situation where an inferior writer with no fuckin' experience whatsoever is writing this book because no one with talent would be caught dead doing so. I think at the time I just liked the sound of "catch-22."

And I'll be up front with you here, before we get into everything. There's a bunch of that crap happening with a mess of writers, not just myself. They'll put some word or phrase in for effect, so it sounds like they know what they're doing, like they're stylistically on top of things. Trust me, they don't, and they aren't.

I just ask one thing from the reader: When I'm struggling to describe people, and can't figure whether to mention the shape of their ears, their foot size, or if they look like a horse, bear with me. I really hate that part of the process, and it shows. I should've just included pictures and a quick bio, saving all parties involved a lot of time and embarrassment.

1

The state of the fire extinguisher was usually a good indicator of what went down on the eleventh floor in Westfall Hall the previous weekend. If you had no recall, n o input, no awareness, or were just away from the dorm for the weekend, a quick glance at the glass casing on Monday morning would furnish a quick overview. It was like the floor barometer. Generally, if glass shards were piled directly below an uncharged extinguisher, the weekend was pretty good. If the pieces were 10 or 20 feet from the point of origin, with the fancy squirt gun empty *and* tossed down the stairs, the weekend was great to excellent. If the soaker was missing altogether it was an outrage: we needed the thing in case a fire broke out for Chrissakes.

The glass that covered the unit was nearly invisible when intact. Very high quality. It fooled many a proud person. Too often an unsuspecting rabble-rouser would attempt a quick snatch of the canister only to be greeted by a miracle force field, three inches from the target. Such a scenario of course would only occur before the weekend reached full bloom. For generally by Saturday, the glass was resoundingly dispatched, usually by violent force. Then the loud footsteps galloping down the hall, then the sound of a huge water jet dousing any fools too slow-witted and/or drunk to figure what was up. They had only themselves to blame, with such a forewarning. Anyone remotely familiar with life on west 11 knew the glass-meets-floor alarm meant canceling existing conversations and leaping for cover in the closest room, no questions asked.

It wasn't like that for the first month of the semester. Most of September was a relatively mellow, docile period, if I recall correctly. No one had to *ever* be on guard, for *anything*. It was a peaceful, idealistic month. Then one Friday night Renny, on a wasted whim, liberated the red can with a bare-fisted shot slicing his knuckle open to the bone. And it kicked off kind of a weekly ritual. Renny enjoyed the act the most, but we all chipped in on an informal rotation. For one thing, it put you on the squirter rather than the squirtee end of the thing, providing benefits too obvious to detail.

Renny got so he could barely accept non-shattered fire extinguisher glass on a Sunday night. He figured out the mathematical equation: intact glass + end of weekend = floor apathy. It was like a loose strand of hair in the mouth for the guy. He patently illustrated this unsettled nature early one Monday morning following an unusually spiritless weekend on the floor. My rapt slumber was dispatched by a sick, misplaced clanking sound, louder than the night was quiet. An apparition, apparently back from taking a leak, then sleepily stumbled through the door, vaulted himself on the top bunk and was snoring again before I could figure what was up. I finally, blearily, pieced together the dark truth: my roommate perpetrated a contrived smashing. The madman didn't want the floor to look bad, bless his heart. I imagine that as he was strolling from the pisser he just slipped the glass a sleepy elbow shot, barely breaking stride. But Renny wasn't alone in his sentimentality. In fact it got so if the fire-extinguisher glass somehow *did* survive the weekend, all the west elevenites in Westfall felt a collective letdown. The norm, however, prescribed a good weekly smashing, and (this is the weird part) by Wednesday the glass was mysteriously repaired, extinguisher charged and shards dutifully swept up, just in time for the weekend festivities. It all seemed to be tied to the entertainment benefits of dorm life, like maintenance of the volleyball court.

*   *   *

I arrived in Fort Collins to attend Colorado State University two years ago, as a second-year transfer student. The town was the last stop of a detoured road trip that originated back East, shot across to Los Angeles where I dropped off my Hawaii-bound brother Graham, then boomeranged back to Colorado. I rolled into the little university town on check-in day at the dorm. The college consumed the place—every person, place or thing seemed somehow tied to its sprawl. I requested a dorm with a good view, so was assigned to the west end of the eleventh floor of Westfall Hall.

I used to ponder this: all the other floors in Westfall were relatively subdued, so why did west 11 overflow with crazed nutcases? But now I'm positive that most of the crazed nutcases *didn't* enter that way. The tone and the mood of the floor simply eventually infected the lot, like a social disease. These souls, for better or for worse, were cast in a mad, frenzied environment, and either scrambled to evacuate while they could, or became mad and frenzied themselves for the full eight-month tenure. I imagine the tenants on the other floors had nearly as disturbing potential. It was no minor sociological phenomenon. Prudence, discretion and uprightness are societal traits that have weathered many a cultural trend. To corral such time-tested values into an ineffective, nearly impotent resistance party on west 11 was no easy undertaking.

All that shit began only four semesters ago, but it seems like eons. It's now my second full summer in Fort Collins—summer jobs are nonexistent here, so I decided to hitchhike out East and back visiting friends; I returned yesterday. It was a great trip, but I'm not going to get into all of that here. I'm presently between my third and forth year in school. AOPers (I said I'll tell you later) generally avoid terms like "sophomore," "junior," etc., as they imply a depressing finiteness to college that most of us refuse to acknowledge. For college to an AOPer is no less than utopia. It's got everything a soul could want—women in their prime, an abundance of drink and song—a more poetic existence couldn't be had. I swear I'm gonna be here forever. Even a fleeting thought of graduation makes me shudder. It makes my hands sweat. It's akin to Linus without his blanket. Hendrix without his guitar. And probably me without a job, with my fucked-up grades.

AOP, incidentally, is short for *The Art of Partying*, kind of a philosophy some of the west elevenites put together while at Westfall Hall. Since I've got more than a month before school fires up again, I figured I'd write a discourse on AOP. Somewhat of a doctoral thesis from someone who probably has a negative-percent chance of receiving a *real* doctorate. Truthfully, there's nothing else to do around here—Fort Collins is a ghost town in the summer. And it's obvious there's a niche for this kind of thing. Check any bookstore: there's a grave shortage of books linking college and rabid partying, for no fathomable reason. It's possibly the most glaring oversight in the hundreds of centuries of literary achievement.

That isn't to say there aren't a host of comprehensive college reference books cluttering up shelves of bookstores across the nation. There are, and each one is loaded with inane statistics like how many frats your favorite college has, how many computer- science degrees were awarded and what the dean's idiot hobbies are. They're actually written for the student's father, knowing he's the one buying the thing. The sad truth is these books ignore the complex realities of college life. They seldom address key inquiries as: "How does one have sex with someone they've just met?" "What are some tried and true methods for passing time during a boring lecture?" "What's one's modus operandi after accidentally passing an audible fart in class?" "Is beer a food?"

Many of the old-school college guides are understandably a bit skittish around more controversial themes, either avoiding them altogether or providing outdated, old-lady-type advice while addressing them. This book bravely takes on such subjects, choosing instead to dissect them like a cadaver in anatomy class. So you get the solutions to these related brainteasers: "How do I party effectively?" "What's the most intelligent manner in which to party?" "How do I put more soul into my partying?" "Why do I hate myself after partying too much?"

Lastly, beyond being a helpful guide, this book waxes poetic on issues of concern to any college student. "Getting Arrested: Character Builder"; "Laundry. Is its 'Inevitability' a Myth?"; "Meditations on Fucking with Authority"; and, essentially, "Being a College Student in the Most Boring, Pathetic, Period of All Time" characterize the subtle tone of these essays.

Granted, as a guide, *College and the Art of Partying* foregoes some practical information. For one thing, it excludes an unabridged list of available colleges in the country and their respective curricula. In fact it makes no reference to any college whatsoever, other than the one I attended. For this reason, the book should be used in conjunction with conventional reference books, rather than as a replacement. As fundamental as *College and the Art of Partying* is to the fledgling student, the book has no intentions on dominating any markets.

In fact, to clarify what the book *does* include, I'm providing my original outline, #1 so the reader knows exactly what the ride will be like, and #2 as a sort of a homage to my first-year English profs. Low-level English professors insist on creating an outline before starting any writing project; I still adhere to this principle three years into my studies. Call it a tribute to the sometimes galling academic traditions which we grudgingly agree benefit us all in the long run.

College and the Art of Partying

I. Preface/Apology/Intro
II. Entering the Dorms
    A. Meeting Roommates
        a. Born-again Christian Splits after Five Days
    B. Meeting the Other Clowns on the Floor
        a. Realizing They're (too) a Bunch of Fuck ups
    C. Some other Shit
III. Dorm Life
    A. The Neurotic Joys the Large Breast Provides
    B. Gleefully Getting Arrested
    C. Really Irresponsible Driving
        a. Enough to Make Most Right-minded Folk Slam the Book Shut in Disgust
    D. Section on Masturbation Placed Before the Driving Section Giving the Right-minded Folk an Out Before They Reach the Driving Section
    E. Section on People and Other Things I Can't Stand
    F. Getting Laid
        a. How and When to do It
    G. Studying
        a. How and when to do it
    H. Getting Laid While You're Studying
        a. That's Impossible
III. Off-Campus Life
    A. Eating on Empty Pockets (other than beer money)
    B. Laundry, Which Really Really Really Blows

IV. Reflections
    A. Honing One's Partying Skills
    B. Guilt-fortified Drivel
V. That's it, Besides a Hoard of other Shit In-between

2

The science of *The Art of Partying* goes like this: In brief, an algorithm was designed whereas each waking moment requires a hedonistic propensity, inherently rejecting conflicting persuasions that revolve around a disproportionately large, guilt-inducing logic core. Which, in layman's terms, of course means, "Tonight we drink, tomorrow we work." This mantra is rooted in the heralded "time transference" equation whereas the "tomorrow," while mere hours away, never actually arrives in its original semantic form, allowing near-uninterrupted partying. The bust in the theory is the day before an exam when it arrives with a vengeance, and you gotta cram for 16 hours straight just to pass.

AOP has no tangibility—it's not a group like a frat, nor is it a treatise espousing a common mindset. There is no countable number of AOP affiliates. It's a Zen-like place existing only in the most committed of partiers, and thus can only be defined obliquely. AOP is the *art* of partying: its dark soul, the nasty depths and teetering heights, the place beyond the outskirts where good and evil come around to meet. It ain't the Greek kid puking his guts after a 12-beer hazing, goes beyond the ritual idiocy of those getting fucked up blindly to escape, and considers any partying experience devoid of social revelation, intellectual stimulation or of course getting one's rock's off just wasted time (so to speak). It's partying's science, its craft; it's the search for the last piece of joy in a lost corner of the world. It's an introduction into all that's unique and restless in your own being, and an initiation deep inside the woman you've just met. It's a nose thumbing at all the inborn tendencies that make one practical, predictable and prosaic. It's betting the pot, spinning the wheel, picking the mad horse; it's the last fuckin' chance before your tedious, worthless life reaches its expiration date.

Very few students are able to fully master AOP. Of course a fierce commitment toward a diverse array of partying principles along with an acute knowledge of the numerous tiers of kicks are necessary. A bulletproof digestive system with a double- walled stomach and iron liver are essential, as is the ability to handle large doses of sleep deprivation. A talent to handily pick up women previously unknown at clubs and parties is a necessity, along with the quality of being able to screw while completely wasted. Even veteran AOPers know the devotion is ongoing and intense. It's also systematic, requiring a mastery of certain skills before moving on. Take the solemn engineering majors always studying on Friday nights: These novices invariably puke after four drinks, i.e. are unable to get past the most basic prerequisite of AOP. Puking not only looks bad, makes the carpet hard the next day, and stinks up the joint, but it wastes alcohol, so there's the irresponsibility factor. And anyone *that* irresponsible sure ain't gonna get too far in a tough field like engineering.

The west side of the eleventh floor in Westfall Hall (you may have guessed) had no engineering majors, that first year at CSU. But it housed a pretty eclectic bunch. By most existing social standards, such a congregation should have been quashed from the onset. A photograph snapped on day one simplistically would have revealed this: a displaced longhair, an urban cowboy, a lame football player, a big maniac with verbal diarrhea, a grinner with bad music and his nondescript roommates, a short apey fellow, a shitty tennis player-turned mushroom head, Kile: The Anti-AOP, two slit-eyed and reclusive potheads, a black guy who somehow resembled a young Burt Reynolds and a bunch of others I'm not gonna mention at the moment.

By comparison, the other floors were great models of uniformity. CSU, nestled in a small, conservative Colorado town, maintained a student body forever juggling the traditional with the progressive. Despite being devoured by a university and all its diversified influences, Fort Collins was still plopped squarely in the heart of America, just a hump in the long sweep of prairies rolling through Northern Colorado, Wyoming and Kansas. Conventional, pragmatic ideologies wafted across the lands and down the halls of the school. Or some halls. Because the phenomenon had little effect on west 11. Somehow, this jumbled array of students quite voluntarily, eventually relinquished most traces of their former orthodox selves. So, while all pictures tell a story, the aforementioned photo aside another snapped eight months later would do no justice to the subjects' metamorphoses. No mere two dimensions could capture the subtle loss of innocence, naïveté and brain cells. Because roughly everyone on west 11 in Westfall Hall underwent some strange alchemic mutation that year. And nearly all flitted in and out of the irregular, funhouse world that was AOP.

3

Westfall Hall has 12 floors. The floor layout consists of two large "U"s bearing 12 rooms on each side, with four elevators framing the dividing lobby. The four corners host suites, which contain two small bedrooms split by a living area, accommodating four students. The other rooms on the floor house two. I was assigned a suite. I arrived around noon on check-in day just after Renny; he seemed all right, so we agreed to share one half of the suite. Renny was a big, barrel-chested affable sort from a small Colorado mountain town who had like 10 siblings. He was a freshman, but looked way older. His getup was checkerboard flannel shirts rolled halfway up the arm, aiming for the rustic, lumberjack look. The guy had mammoth hands. Unfortunately, the fingers on these hands housed some *massive* warts which he'd try to remedy with a pocketknife. It made what was just a bad situation grisly. And it guaranteed that whenever around him, your eyes would make constant updates on the state of his limbs, in uncontrollable fashion.

Renny, I discovered quickly, was a talker beyond belief. Or at least when it came to certain subjects. I personally am a failure at small talk. And if attempted while sober, it's sometimes so forced, it feels as if I'm *lying* or something while I'm doing it. It's pretty bizarre. But this suited Renny, giving him all the more room to operate. The subject he adored, cherished, *lived for*, was this family feud involving his relatives and the neighbors across the street. I'd relate the details to you, but they're so dull, you'd seal up the book maybe for good. Anyway, I mainly recall his bellowing tones and exaggerated facial expressions. Renny, with the conviction of a holy man, could spin this yarn like a goddamned tornado. And Lord it was interminable.

During my and Ren's first 30 minutes of conversation, he baited me like a seasoned pro. Requisite exchanges of brief life histories out of the way, he began to take the monologue and shake it like a rug, until the only thing ultimately worth discussing was the family feud. He toyed with me like a child, circling the topic with tighter and tighter spirals of oration. He offhandedly mentioned the feud a number of times, adeptly weaving it in and out of a number of different stories. Sometimes it blended in nicely, other times it was clunkily misplaced. Around the fifth time he mentioned it, during an innocuous skiing anecdote, I bit, and bit hard. "So what's this family feud thing?"

I should have seen it coming. I was like a fly motoring smack into the spider web. Renny discarded the worthless present story like some dirty dishwater. His eyes got as big as beer coasters. He began to sweat, and clop back and forth in the chair. Then he stood up. He didn't even need the fuckin' chair! He frothed and foamed; words were jettisoned from his mouth. He ripped into the family feud business, nearly knocking me over. Offshoot asides were juggled haphazardly with the central theme; these in turn spawned even more trivial digressions. Nothing could halt such a runaway train—no half-lidded looks of boredom—even completely ignoring him fazed him none. Fifteen minutes into the thing I picked up the song jacket to a Big Head Todd CD, and memorized every lyric on it. His mind processed the act differently, perceiving it instead as me staring at him in rapt wonder. I couldn't deny his mastery of longevity: only a split second divided his sentences, deftly sealing off interjections. Finally, maybe hours down the line, I somehow inserted "thatwasoneheckofastory" at a potential cut-off spot, causing him to frown and scoff at this small, pathetic effort to get him to stop. He was just getting his second wind, dammit. Old Renny might have continued clear until morning, until I was a dusty old skeleton, but, like a gift from heaven, another roommate appeared.

Renny glared over his shoulder at the poor-excuse-of-an-interruption. Colin was its name. I hadn't been so happy to see someone in a decade. I immediately became acutely interested in subjects like his hometown and his major, minor and any fallback majors and minors. I had to build a wall of words to keep Renny at bay. And believe it, for *me* that's a lot of work

Colin was a born-againer, it turned out. He subtly broke it to us after removing his jacket, which displayed a tee shirt that read something like "Repent or Burn for Eternity." It had an artist's rendition of hell on it. It saddened me, watching his sweaty toilings. Unpacking, hooking up the stereo, fiddling with the television antennae, sticking a poster up—in a matter of days he'd be applying the very same energies, but in reverse. It seemed like a waste of human effort. The poor lad would be driven out by the Satanists themselves, and of course, he'd tell his Christian buddies, it was all for a reason— *everything* has a goddamned reason. And the reason was that he couldn't party worth a runny shit. It's that simple. Then Tyce showed up.

He appeared silently and stood at the room's entrance for a full minute, like a cowboy witnessing the city for the first time. He was a presence. Tall with a dark complexion and a mustache, he donned a cream-colored ten-galloner that made him stoop to avoid hitting the top of the doorway. "Home" is all he said, eventually. He ambled in with the conscious gait all cowboys seem to have. I immediately lamented that a redneck was planted in my suite; he side-eyed the longhaired, tanned, surfer-type who must have gotten off the wrong plane in cattle country.

"I'm Mick," I said, and then introduced the other two. It was a ridiculous gesture, considering I knew them for all of an hour. After quick hellos, Tyce moseyed to the music collections, determining what he'd gotten himself into. Renny all this time stayed pathologically silent, watching the scene like a cat. Colin sat nervously out of harm's way. Tyce went up the stack then down it, in full crouch. The music didn't seem to impress the newcomer, a very, very poor first sign. The entire display of 300 CDs, records and tapes were surveyed without comment. It was worrisome. The stereo was to be the fifth roommate—and the most cherished—and if the others objected to her presence, trouble would ensue. He next saddled over to the books. Nietzsche, Thurber, Kafka, Camus—none elicited a remark. "If you're looking for Billy the Kid's biography, don't waste your time," I was thinking. "Shit, let's all get some beer," I said.

We bought a case and headed back to the room. The brew loosened everyone up. Tyce turned out to be cool as ice, and I felt guilty for tagging the stereotype. His full name was Tyson; he chose the short form with a "c." He spent his first two college years at Hayes State in Kansas, and followed his parents' move to Colorado to continue receiving in-state tuition. When he talked, his dark eyes were never skittish or wavering—they burned a hole in the bridge of your nose. Tyce seemed to manner extreme confidence blended with a good dash of Midwestern naiveté. When he'd encounter an off-center thought, he'd convey a strange, old-fashioned bemusement. His brow would wrinkle while it processed in his mind, determining if it bore reasonability or not. Throughout high school and college the guy had been a mother's dream—he was an "A" student and a scholarship football player at Hayes until a shoulder injury put him down.

"Dya mind?" Tyce queried Renny, pointing at the smokes. He shifted the cold cigarette around in his mouth for a good 10 minutes.

"They're better if you light 'em."

"No man, I never smoke," he said, then reconsidered, and lit it up. And he's smoked ever since. It was a curious scene, and maybe an instant turning point for Tyce, the first spark of a life primed for an overhaul. For as the beer flowed and guards were dropped, the guy appeared surreally contradictory—mannering homespun, Midwestern ideals that were his makeup, while showing keen interest in all that violated them. The Doors' "Strange Days" was playing, and getting turned up a notch for every beer downed. "This record's too trippy," Tyce decided, who then pored over the full lyric sheet. It seemed in this short introduction that Tyce, at the ripe age of 20, had tired of the images his life had come across. And that it was high time for him to do something about it.

It was a good thing to witness, especially from this guy I had boxed away the first minute I met him. I mean, who worth a damn wouldn't choose to enter school in similar fashion? Hell, we were in college—great redefinitions were in store for us all.

A few pisses later, the dorm had reached full capacity. I took a slow lap around the floor, watching as the temporary domiciles were assembled. It was impossible at this stage to figure whether the people passing were to be some thorn in the side, lifelong friends or sad ghosts of indifference. The mind, however, wired for simplicity, nosily processes its own verdict. It takes a 12-word exchange with some clown at the water fountain and without consent registers the impression, compares it with other data in the memory bank and files it away before the poor soul knows what hit him.

Of course these cursory observations require future updatings and refinements. But oddly, sometimes they're right on. Andre, for example, could be entirely figured out in one brief visit. He saved all people he came across a good deal of brainpower in the long run. At this point I was six-beers friendly, and stuck my head in his room to introduce myself. Andre was sticking up the September Playboy centerfold; he'd refresh it in a month. "I can't stand these silicone-injected tits," he reported, carefully assuring they were perpendicular to the floor. He was a small, hairy fellow with a scrappy, bird-nest beard. He had the face of a little ape. If his arms were longer he seriously could have worked in a zoo. His look obliged him to act impish and quirky and humorous. Trouble is, it was done popular-opinion style. He memorized hundreds of comedic slogans and phrases afloat in the mainstream of popular culture, and splashed his conversation with them. And when of course no laughs resulted, *you'd* get accused of not having the sense of humor.

Andre employed a classic character of compensation. From where I stood, it appeared as rigorous work. I asked where he was from; he said New Jersey, while stuffing some Copenhagen in his bottom lip. It clarified that although his birth certificate said Jersey, his heart was true to ol' Coloradi. He'd respond to questions dually, to the asker and to some crazy inner debate of his own. The scrawny little guy somehow worked in after six sentences some anecdote of his days as a boxer. I suppose it was to account for his obvious spindlyness, in hopes he'd appear more scrappy than spindly. Except his timing was so bungled and unsubtle, he exited the story actually looking spindlier than ever. He actually dropped pounds in a mere 10 minutes of conversation.

There's no fighting the mind's need for order, as it dutifully organizes complete strangers into types. But following this sterile process, it's one's civic duty to allow the individual a quick get-away from this very restricting first impression. One way is to take your end of the dialogue and bend, twist or color it, demanding that the personality opposite you react distinctly and freely. It's like opening the door to the mouse cage. Lots of mice will break for freedom, never to be seen again. But others, like Andre, simply stay put in the cage. They steadfastly choose life as a derivative being. The rationale makes some sense I suppose: it's akin to riding in a life that's already been test-driven. But it's weird conversing with these sorts. You get so many senses of deja vu, it's like re-watching a fuckin' video for the hundredth time.

The thing about mouse people is that folks *outside* the cage likewise bug the balls off of *them*. They're constant reminders of their own mouse-like state. Rusty down the hall was a mouse person for a couple months, upon arrival. He entered CSU with the demeanor of a third-string high school tennis player, which he'd happened to be. *His* first-impression system was straight out of a book. His third sentence to me was, "So do you do a lot of drugs?" I reckon he saw the long hair and disparagingly deduced that I belonged in the druggie/poor-athlete classification. So I took great pleasure during the next day's volleyball game in smashing a 70 mph spike to the side of his head, at least clearing up the half of it. He found it a painful lesson in brainless stereotyping. But Rusty cooled considerably, eventually shook free of himself, and became a good friend.

(I have no explanation why) but one thing's certain about these apple pie types like ex-Rusty entering college, the great traditional-value holders and the staunch abstainers of mind-altering stimuli: *they're* the ones you end up worrying about. Because when they invariably *do* indulge in drugs and alcohol, they generally overdo them, I guess making up for lost time. Rusty, a prime example, by sophomore year was chomping 'shrooms weekly. Basic sanity in these turbulent times is tenuous enough—no need to be toying with whatever's left like *that*.

Making the rounds, I stumbled onto Rich and Tim, who lived next to Andre. The two were childhood friends from Boulder. In celebration of their first full day of emancipation, the embarkment of a nascent phase in life, they got irreparably stoned. And, more troubling, they weren't social stoners. When I greeted them, they wore the easily spotted spare-me-from-social-confrontation look in their reddened eye. Feeling beer-ish and gregarious, I didn't.

Now, it's common knowledge that the six-beer mindset and the stoned mindset are natural enemies, but I was out to prove a peaceful coexistence was possible. Having a good journeyman's knowledge of stonedness, I knew it would involve honing in on the salvageable areas of their mental states and making connections in an unobtrusive, unintimidating manner. Cued by their music, I began practically, offering the fellows a theory that Pink Floyd is perhaps the most underrated band in rock due to the band's lousy choice of an anachronistic name. Could any altered mindset, regardless of severity, not respond to hypotheses on Pink Floyd? Indeed; it happened in this very instance. Rich and Tim in fact were incapable of anything apart from automatic functions of the body, like breathing, sneezing and farting. They tried to assemble apologetic looks on their faces; they even screwed *that* up. They looked more like they were in mourning. It's a curious endeavor—purposefully getting that ripped, then thrashing and struggling for hours trying to re-gather one's marbles. Over time, Rich and Tim turned out to be interesting people, but if you wanted to party with them, it oddly had to be in the safety of their room. In fact I never saw them leave the stupid place. They had a full semester's supply of pot and music, so really saw no need to. On many a rough day, one could see their point.

4

One's initial impression of Wilt had to be this: he was an extremely happy sort. Wilt's a big, husky dude, who lived across the hall. He forever's got grin pinned to his face. I later realized the smile was independent of mood. Wilt smiles when nervous, upset, napping, glad, brushing his teeth—always. His hair goes every which way, like a semi-straightened Afro, also regardless of disposition.

I met Wilt at a floor party the first weekend in the dorms, during a good-natured confrontation over the music. I had the reigns of the CD player, and was drunkenly pumping out the most fanatical, non-dance-friendly music I could muster. I wanted to get a rise out of everyone, to see what made these Midwesterners tick. During Hendrix' "The Star Spangled Banner," Wilt popped by and innocently requested "Celebration," by Kool and the Gang. It struck me as obscenely funny at the moment. I wasn't sure if the human ear was meant to handle such opposing sounds side by side. I suggested we work up to it with a careful transition, like through a Prince buffer or something.

Wilt was a freshman at CSU, and was unable to fully shake certain freshman-like characteristics for a good quarter semester. Thus, he initially came off as cautious, a bit cliquey, regimented. It would've been a poor bet that this bad-music liking person who considered Tyce and me unsavory for drinking before the sun went down would eventually become the CEO of AOP, if there was one. In a remarkably short time the man evolved into one of the finest partiers on campus: his music became tolerable to very good, his guilt eradication was as honed as anyone's, and he posed no restrictions on drinking (other than a flexible no-shots-before-breakfast policy). I've always believed he could have turned professional if his stomach was a bit stronger. For on brief occasion, Wilt's digestive tract would fail him, demanding a break from the festivities without further discussion. It's a bleak, sorrowful sight. Witnessing a fellow like Wilt in the nasty throes of sobriety during the lunacy of spring-break week is a tragic thing. It's like watching a wounded, grounded bird helplessly hopping around in the parking lot.

Wilt's eventual mastery of AOP coincided with a newfound desire to explore untapped areas of his personality. This was accomplished generally through drinking, and the result was a full personality conversion. He didn't just toe these fresh waters, he plunged in headlong, then went down in the whirlpool. His drinking and non-drinking selves were like mutant twins. They were so opposite in nature, they'd barely nod to each other in the elevator. Yet both resided within Wilt, who expertly mediated the situation. And all three coexisted generally without incident.

Depending on his plans for the day, Wilt would determine which half he'd let come out and play. If his schedule included attending classes, shooting hoops, studying or sleeping, he'd enlist Mr. Sober, who kind of showed up by default. Mr. Sober handled all ordinary, everyday tasks well enough, but when it came to partying, he was like a virgin trying to make it on a waterbed. Wilt's Mr. Sober was all thumbs at picking up girls, pissing out of eleventh-floor windows or falling down stairs. And the fact was somewhat embarrassing, especially for the foremost partier on campus. So for these roles, Wilt'd summon Mr. Souse, who'd only rouse if he were fed whiskey, tequila or beer. Every weekend, out of necessity, Wilt'd diligently pack a suitcase for the mellow, introverted Mr. Sober, and send him a long, long way away. Somehow the poor joker would find his way back on Monday morning, right before class.

Most of the AOP heavies were good athletes; Wilt was easily the best. He was a natural, commanding any sport he preferred yet had no traces of an idiot-jock, herd mentality. Not one minute was ever wasted by Wilt or any AOPer watching sports on television. I suppose it was considered insultingly vicarious. In fact, nearly every media form was oddly vanquished. It wasn't evident until months down the line, but dorm life slowly and strangely became life in a vacuum. While many of us were staunch readers, the newspaper was generally disregarded. Movies were never attended, TV and videos absolutely never watched and professional sports all but ignored. So any gains in academic and social education were somewhat offset by a complete obliviousness of the prevailing culture.

But it took an insular world like this for AOP to flourish. Despite the fact that AOP was often a puerile, unrefined and socially despicable world, it at least was one of our own construct. And even though a chunk of it seemed determined to take a mindless, random dump on respectability and reason, the brunt of AOP seemed to deliver new meaning and potential. It was the fresh poetry of the skid row denizen versus the tired redraft of the uptown suit. After all, what's the point of the so-called freedom and independence of college life if it's all within someone else's design?

Still, it's difficult to escape the droning influence of Practical Choices and of Solidly Mapped-Out Futures, especially in today's college climate. And without the promise of AOP, any one of us on west 11 could have gotten swept up in that crap. 'Cause Christ, it seems where ever you go in college, *someone's* got a plan for you.

Parents mean well, and of course want the very best for their kids. Minimally, they desire that a good, well-adjusted citizen emerges from the university. Some are pushier than that, and force-feed various careers down their kids' throats. Whatever their methods, it's clear parents mainly want a kid worth bragging about in the Christmas letter.

One thing's for certain: few parents dream their kid masters the Art of Partying in college. The harried, nutso world of AOP counters the very grain of a parent's being. For way back on one's zero-th birthday, when the parents are born, they take on a mysterious manifestation, known as the "My Baby!" syndrome. The "My Baby!" syndrome is a mind-set that's fiercely suspicious of anything that might cause My Baby! harm, and it's carried to an obsessive level by the fledgling parents. Risk-loving, carefree sorts develop the incurable affliction the moment they reproduce. And the resulting mutation is a perversely dull, speed-limit-driving champion of innocence, replete with full memory loss of all pre-baby days.

This state of mind is somewhat antithetic to the offspring-free, let's-get-wasted-and-laid philosophy of the university student. So, despite their excellent intentions, parents' wishes for even their college-aged kids are severely at odds with reality.

Society's desires for the student are a bit more ominous. Actually, if you pick one of the majors listed in the college catalogue, particularly Criminal Justice, then decide to practice it upon graduation, society generally won't mess with you. But if you choose to study the Art of Partying, you'll join its 205,163 semi-most-wanted list. Mainstream society to an AOPer is like the stern schoolmaster rapping your knuckles every time you do something that pisses her off. And she's such a prudish, unbending old bid, who can help but rearing back and goading her yet again?

Actually, society is weirder than just an uptight old bid. It's an uptight old bid you can't even hear or see—just a watered-down, harping mass-opinion wafting throughout the minds of its 300 million constituents.

And for an AOPer, that's kind of the problem. Anything tailored to work for 300 million assholes is going to provide the individual about as much kicks and enlightenment as the local merry-go-round.

It's a confusing situation for newly emancipated college students, working to reconcile their fresh convictions with the stale ones of an invisible, mute, uptight curmudgeon. The lines between right and wrong become blurred, a less-objective morality is created and numerous ethical questions are raised. For example, many west elevenites had struggled with this conundrum: Say 10 AOPers decided to use an open eleventh-floor-lobby window for a urinal on late weekend nights. And say this was done so regularly, so unthinkingly, that late-night window pissing developed into a virtual norm. Now consider 10 people on a dorm committee promoting their own norm by sealing up all dorm-lobby windows in response, like a prison. The ethical issue is this: can one arbitrary norm necessarily be considered more "correct" than another?

Unfortunately, after analyses, it would seem so. The dorm committee contended that first and foremost, people mulling in the courtyard below have the basic right not to get peed on. They also concurred that this manner of relieving one's self is unsightly, sets a poor example, and can stain the carpet and erode the windowsill with the end-of-stream dribble. In conclusion, they believed the act was also illegal, deviant and probably worthy of therapy. And our argument? We didn't really have one. We used the shoddy defense that drunkenly watching a piss stream cascade downwards for 11 stories was pleasing. Aside their robust stand, our position seemed vacuous and foolish. And worse, all of their points seemed to ring true, except maybe the crack about us needing therapy.

As I mentioned, college can be a confusing experience. Especially when some of the finest moments of one's life can so easily be linked to irrationality, abhorrence and psychoanalysis. The student is relegated to a misunderstood, indefensible minority pitted against a host of social mores and legislated laws conjured by the dorm-administration-10 and

300 million equally logical sorts. And this minefield of laws and rules of conduct explodes regularly in the adventurous student's face.

But the minefield metaphor certainly doesn't hold true for all students. For example, Wilt's roommates Darrell, Gerry and Chuck viewed laws and rules of conduct more as guideposts, security blankets. And they pretty much entered CSU with nearly all of them memorized. They had terrific memories. These guys' destinies seemed to be lessons in adaptation, in survival tactics. Unlike a lot of the west elevenites, they saw little need to edit the pages of the world they encountered. Their preferences were to blend in—if they had it their way they'd have worn camouflage suits. One got the impression they could hang with us or with a frat or anywhere. Since they were ill-fatedly tossed on the west side of the eleventh floor, they were forced to adjust to a debased world of too much drinking and lots of free sex. But it was funny with Darrell, Gerry and Chuck. Their powers of compliance were so well honed they too became respectable partiers, at least during their stint on 11. So they did okay by the Art of Partying. You'd technically still have to call it conformity, but with a sick, dark twist to it all.

5

Dorm life is often castigated by upperclassmen, who find the close quarters and lack of privacy a great liability. And it's true there are as many bodies per capita in the dorms as in the local prison. But the tightly insulated environment has a strong upside: it's an absolutely peerless social forum. Even a hermit can't help but entangled himself in its odd web of humanity.

    It didn't take long to figure out that of the 12 floors on Westfall, the even- numbered ones were spilling with females. Essentially, it was the job of the residents of the odd-numbered floors to get in the pants of those on the even floors or vice versa. That's dorm life in a nutshell. The first thing noticeable when venturing on the even-numbered floors was that they were physically intact: no broken glass cluttering the hallways, no beer-and-vomit scented carpets, no punched-in ceilings and no passed-out people in the lobbies. These were floors true to architectural intentions. Sauntering down the pristine corridors an implicit understanding occurred: that behind all the neatly rowed doors were women in their physical prime, with gorgeous, naked bodies just beneath their clothes. Now college students, they were primed to reject the survival techniques of the past, depart from the universal mind and blossom into distinct creatures. In high school only a few types of girls can be found; college houses thousands. Their personalities fragment and mutate the second they step on campus. It's a remarkable transformation.

But there are many levels of intimacy in this restless, tightly packed congregation. On any given night, thousands of reasons not to study exist. People are jammed in shoulder to shoulder; human interactions are demanded. Doors are left ajar, inviting passersby to stop in for a smoke, a beer or to resume a dialogue unfinished from the night before. An army of stereos vie for attentions. The prevailing song muscles its way down the hall, brazenly interjecting its own discussion and causing subconscious alterations of idea or presentation. Environmental interplays are forever occurring. And they involve a great variety of mental states at their most adventurous, their most free and their most animated. College is the rare, flashing period where nothing doesn't exist—the proverbial "dream" is full and brimming with hope. A great allowance of change is finally possible—students are at last able to shed their birth skin and design their own, inside and out. Conversation, manner assume a novel, fearless quality—the soul apart from family, former peer groups, and other signs of familiarity reacts like a newly freed prisoner. "Life shall begin at this moment and its reinvention shall be holy." It's wonder, plainly put.

The surest way to gauge a new dorm acquaintance is through his or her CD collection. It's kind of like a Rorschach test without the inkblots and spontaneous responses. Ninety percent of a person's personality can be assembled in this manner. Certain collections display works of a timeless, lasting character; others are replete with faddish, fading hits of the moment. Some are gathered in strong-willed assuredness; others compiled plainly for the approval of others. The days of finding someone without a sizable music collection are gone. Even the uncoolest computer geek on earth has a large collection to pop in his computer while he's jerking to the Tit's and Beaver web site. A towering CD display is also one way people with zero sense of abstract appreciation can loosely conceal it. Trouble is, it's written all over their collection. Recording companies in fact now employ a host of musicians who create CDs for conflicted sorts who dislike music but require a huge wall of discs to display in their dorm room.

Wilt's feeble offering of dance music interspersed with a decently sized section of shit rock was an inauspicious beginning for a young man embarking on a college career. His tastes were far from incorrigible however; they in fact improved substantially over the semester. He along with Tyce in time became as rabid a Doors fan as anyone. But it took him a few months to complete the transition. During this period, it was a mystery how the musical section of his brain worked. It would cue him to blast a shit-laced Madonna CD, then toss on a masterpiece like The Doors' "The End," and follow it all up with that fuckin' disco song where they're singing about a roller coaster. It defied logic. I came to realize down the line that "the song" was in fact secondary to Wilt. What turned him on was how a tune sounded on his expensive stereo. If the trebles, midranges and basses were blended in sonic perfection, it didn't matter to him if a Gregorian chant was rocking the place.

It quickly became evident that sound systems played an integral role in dorm life. With all the new faces and eclectic personalities thrown together in such jammed living quarters, determining territorial dominance early on was a necessity. This was established of course by the stereo, and my and Wilt's outfits quashed all nearby contenders. Any formidable system's music space should cover at least a full horizontal floor of a dorm (with the host door open); with windows ajar the sound should also raid around four vertical floors on a windless day. Such sound space seldom goes unchallenged, however.

My stereo pumped out a few more decibels than Wilt's; his had a slight edge on overall clarity. Like a cruel joke however, his system was somehow devoid of fused speakers, and when really cranked the pricey tweeters would often fry like a piece of bacon. Thus, with my assistance, it eventually developed a reputation as a jazz outfit, much to Wilt's disappointment. Our rooms were aptly situated in the corners of the "U," facing each other. At 10 and some odd paces apart, a daily duel was inevitable.

The event, nearly from day one, would transpire as follows: After a long, tiring day at classes the eleventh floor elevator doors would part and I'd get a sour, unwelcome greeting of thumping dance music, which caused a sharp pain in my belly. Opening the door to the hallway the sound would increase three-fold, the place fully awash in offensive noise. I'd sprint towards my room, fumble for a Jimi Hendrix CD, and direct the volume control to seven-and-a-half. The Hendrix music would mightily push the offensive noise backwards, effectively corralling it back into its room of origin, limiting its floor presence. After a few minutes the offensive noise would pause between songs, and Wilt, realizing his system was being bullied, would leap up and counter with a daring right twist of the dial, secretly praying his effeminate tweeters would survive it. At this point the noise caused the music to retreat a bit, and sonic ranges became equidistant from their respective stereos. It was a poor fate, but Rusty and his roommate Kile's room was situated exactly at midpoint, right where the two sounds collided. Here, a state of sonorousness occurred which was ugly beyond belief. It miffed Wilt and me that they survived the entire year without cracking up.

6

Our suitemate Colin, as expected, didn't last a week. Although endless nights of music screaming at 3 a.m. coupled with a steady diet of women, booze and pot might sound like nirvana to the typical college student, it was enough for Colin to plan a speedy relocation. On his last day, while he was hastily packing his belongings, he accidentally knocked over someone's eight-month old bong water on his pillow, causing a smell-stain that is pretty-much permanent. So even his sleeping moments were to be invaded by the west 11 nightmare. Colin didn't just move to another room; he arranged a residence on the far side of campus. He ensured that the student center, a lagoon, the liberal-arts building, numerous trees and a half mile separated the two dormitories.

Not a day after Colin departed, Don Barnes, who lived a few doors down, came knocking. Don was a mellow, shaggy fellow who was on a football scholarship. He was far removed from the typical football jock though; quite the antithesis actually. For Don was a cool cat. AOP puts a high standard on "cool," relegating the category to only a handful of people. Don was a near fit. He displayed the restraint of behavior and economy of word and demeanor that coolness requires. And he not once expended a surplus of effort in anything he did. Don desired to fill the Colin vacancy. "My roommate likes to study a lot," was his rationale. He never over-explained anything. I figured Tyce would be reluctant, as he had the ideal dorm situation—a half suite to himself. But knowing we could arbitrarily be assigned another Colin, we okayed the request, and Don became our latest suitemate. Don, at around six-foot-two, was the shrimp of the group. When the four of us were standing in the middle living area, it looked like one of those optical illusion fun-house rooms with a too-low ceiling and too-narrow walls.

A few days after Don settled in, his ex-roommate Steven passed Tyce and me in the hall. His brow had a worried, furrowed quality to it. "Have you seen Don around?" he wondered. Don of course had failed to mention the move to the lad.

Before September was over, Don injured his knee, pretty much ending his football career. With the extra free time, he came up short on excuses for bombing his classes. He'd rise in the morn before any of us, and comb the campus trying to track down recruits to take his tests and quizzes for him. He wasn't without a smooth delivery, and was able muster a few volunteers here and there. Of course come crunch time they'd get cold feet, realizing their college careers were on the line. This puzzled old Don. Aware of his massive efforts, his faithful roomies would request regular updatings. "What's the scoop on that Econ test next Monday, man?"

"Everybody keeps backing out!" he'd blurt in exasperation.

Don took laziness to another level. It was an expertise. While all our rooms were essentially large laundry baskets that required wading through a foot of dirty clothes, his ample wardrobe actually created a barrier from one side of his room to the other. The far side by the window was walled off, virtually inaccessible. Tyce easygoingly went along with it. The two just adapted to living with the objects in three-quarters of the room.

Early in the fall semester, the college had to do some construction work by the dorm bike racks, and gave everyone a month's notice to displace the cycles. Those still chained would have the locks cut and would be stored in a locked room in the basement. Don couldn't find the time to move his bike of course, nor could he muster the energy to ask someone to retrieve the cycle later shackled in the storeroom. Every two months when we'd do laundry downstairs Don would find his way to the locked room, put his face against the door and longingly whisper, "biiiiike."

Without wheels, the poor guy had to had to hoof it everywhere. One night he and I embarked on a trek for beer, and wended down the pathway beside the dorm. As we rounded the corner, we came across a pizza delivery guy. As he squeezed past us on the narrow sidewalk, Don reeled and farted a dandy exactly on the pizza man. The fellow seemed confused as to whether an assault had taken place or not. At that point, a brand new facial expression was created. But Christ, how can anyone get too worked up over a fart??

Don came to college with his girlfriend Cammie in tow, a thin, long-legged girl with a cheerleader's body. She was sweet and foxy, but also suspicious of this den of thieves Don was now amongst. It was obvious she'd have her hands full. The first weekend following Don's arrival, Cammie burst into the bedroom where Tyce was heavily engaged with a pick-up. "Donald you bastard!!" she screamed, flicking on the lights, scaring the bejesus out of Tyce's friend. After she left in embarrassment, the naked girl gathered her wits and remarked, "Hey, you said your name was Tyce!"

It *is* a fact that getting laid in the dorms occurs not without some planning. The basic strategy involves finding a date and beating your roomie back to your side of the suite on the weekends, so you can lock his ass out. A just situation occurs when both parties party late, with equal fervor. Renny soon, however, unfairly began staying in on weekends, defending our side of the suite like a security guard. You'd have to lurk in the stairwell with your chick, then rush the door while he stepped out for a leak. This would prompt Renny to reciprocate a full lockout days later when he'd just be *talking* to a chick in there. The poor bastard had so many deformed warts covering his hands I can't imagine any woman *ever* letting him touch her. It's frightening to even discuss. But suite-life offered the great advantage of a central area with a couch, accommodating the odd man out. My van was available in double lockout emergencies, having a bed in the back. Though the van was seldom necessary, the room seemed to always have some unlucky fool crashed on the couch.

Whacking off in the dorms requires as much creativity as getting laid. There's simply no reasonable place to beat the meat. It's an inherent flaw in the dorm's setting. Early morning is the safest time, using a sock under the covers while you're "still sleeping." When the discreetness of the technique is mastered, 10 people can be filing in and out completely oblivious to what's going on. The tough part is maintaining composure during orgasm. But it only works when sober, when you don't need huge piston strokes to produce.

Later in the day it gets tougher. Showers are generally community in the dorms, thus are off limits. The floor shitter is an option but everyone in the dorm knows it, and guilt is automatically assumed after a 10 minute odorless "crap." Spurting after a smelly dump is much more logical. Branching away from the dorm is yet another alternative. The library is a natural spot for makin' gravy, since it's natural to desire to offset the pain of reading metaphysics for the last hour with a good old hedonistic whack off. Glamour or Cosmopolitan magazines work sufficiently—you can nearly always find at least a topless chick somewhere in there. Finding a deserted bathroom isn't that difficult, however if someone comes in you've gotta abort, which epitomizes frustration when you're 20 seconds from shooting. And for all the macho idiots out there who say "I don't jerk off—I just get laid"—they're either chock full of shit, or surely the lousiest lays on earth. 'Cause if you got a month's worth of that shit built up, when you *do* find a chick you're gonna spurt after 20 strokes no matter how many beers you've had. Anyone too hung up or embarrassed to whack off has got some nasty psychological guilt-trip shit going on, and probably isn't a good candidate for this book to begin with.

As a side note, males universally wonder why females, with no boners to hide or jism burdens, masturbate as infrequently as they do. Trust me, I've discussed this with hundreds of women. It all makes zero sense. The only thing keeping us from whacking 24 hours a day is such restrictions. Imagine being able to sit on the plane, slide your hand under the blanket on your lap and get off with total inconspicuousness. Or to do the same while driving in your car. Boring, tedious trips to the supermarket would exist no more. Yet most women, inexplicably, squander this awesome gift. And those who don't, seldom solo-pilot for the sake of pure physical pleasure. They gotta create this whole fantastic fantasy journey in their heads, with the right mood, candles, incense, a *bathtub*— the works. The setup itself takes 15 goddamned minutes. It messes with the spontaneous hedonism of the act. All *we* need is a picture of some stretchmarkless tits and a bottle of Jergins. Hell, even the Jergins isn't mandatory. But there is something kind of noble in the female approach to masturbation. I mean, as long as they're doing it *somehow*. 'Cause if they aren't, they're wasting human anatomy.

7

September and January are special months for the college student. They're gateway months, invitations into the new semester. They're beacons of academic light seen in the distance by those who are coming off a summer vacation, terminating a winter break or entering for the first time the hallowed grounds of the university. AOPers are doubly appreciative of these times of year, because they're optimal partying periods. No one's behind on assignments, and no major tests loom in the near future. So the partying is ongoing and accomplished guilt-free, unlike the cruel months of December and May.

The following graph indicates the relationship between partying and studying in a typical fall term. The same graph can be transposed to spring semester, also.

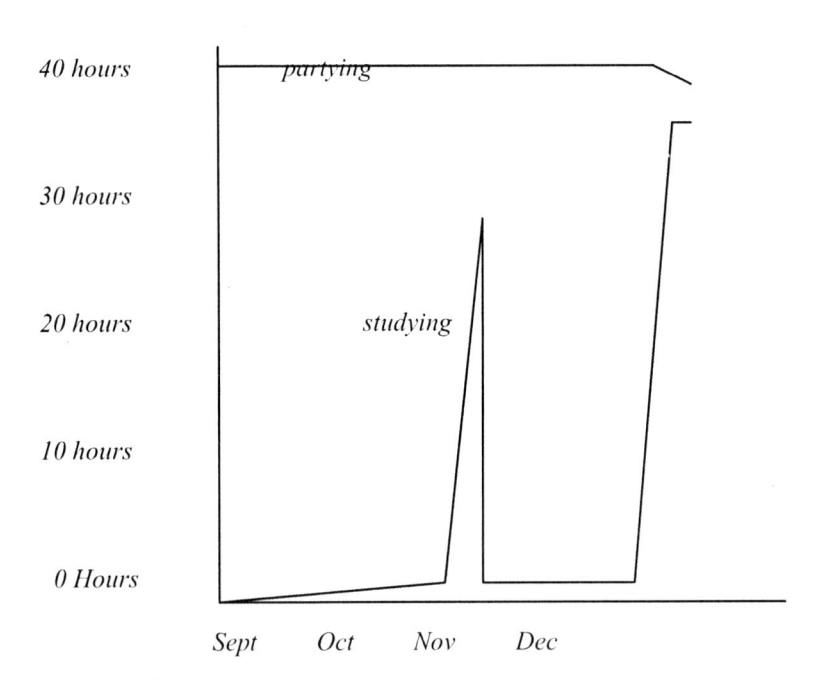

```
40 hours  ┌──── partying ──────────────────┐
                                           │
                                           │
30 hours                                   │
                             ┐             │
                             │             │
20 hours         studying    │             │
                             │             │
                             │             │
10 hours                     │             │
                             │             │
                             │             │
 0 Hours  └──────────────────┘─────────────┘

          Sept    Oct    Nov    Dec
```

Note: *The atypical mid-semester studying spike accounts for midterm exams.*

Partying in September also is an accelerated way of unveiling the mishmash of personalities tossed together in a dorm. It's quite possible to condense three months of slow, methodical acquaintance into two good, drunken all-nighters. It's like a speed-reading course in social behavior. Political philosophies, books read, musical influences—all that shit comes gurgling from the mouth after just a few shots and a truckload of beer.

Such raucous all-nighters originated in our dorm room, 1111, and flamed outward toward key sites scattered throughout west 11. The other rooms housed innocent victims. The victims' objections and formal complaints regarding the round-the-clock stereos and other high-decibel activity petered out after a month or so. Don placated most complainants with a hypnotically repeated mantra: "The dorms aren't for studying. The library is for studying." It was the entire text to his side of the debate. Come 3:00 a.m. when we'd return from a long night of partying to crank the stereo at full volume, Don logically expanded the maxim to, "The dorms aren't for sleeping. The library is for sleeping." And it was true about the library. I for one can barely keep my eyes open in the joint.

So from October on, partying took on an unbroken, purist form. Even the Resident Assistant had a blind eye to the goings on. In fact he took one long look at the unseemly group at the get-to-know-ya meeting the first day, then retreated to his abode on the opposite side of the floor, never to be seen again. East 11, which was past the elevators, housed another reality altogether. It reeked strongly of mass studymanship and law and order. Besides the Resident Assistant, hoards of self-respecting engineers and other folk too nondescript to mention dotted east 11. A couple guys like James and Tom could party elementarily, but they faltered miserably when attempting to meet AOP standard. Venturing on our side of the floor after dark, they looked like greenhorns the first day on a ranch. I also remember some guy over there named Vince. As far as the others—I don't think most of us knew any of their names. There's a possibility they didn't even *have* names.

Somewhat surprisingly, our roommate Tyce seemed right at home in the west 11 madness. In fact, some quick things were discovered about the fellow, which belied his well-groomed first impressions. For starters, his libido was remarkably hyperactive. We'd be partying in the room, preparing to head to a party, and he'd take off for the pisser. Not necessarily intentionally, he'd too-often return with a smitten girl in the same amount of time as any un-detoured leak. A hello and an invitation for a beer was the approximate effort involved. Not long after, he'd find an excuse for the two to slip into his side of the suite, whereas both parties' resistances quickly deteriorated. When they'd later emerge, he'd jump right back into the conversation like he was back from getting a beer. It was all done matter-of-factly, with no trace of macho bravado. Very coolly, it wasn't a huge deal for anyone, and thus was never degrading or embarrassing to his partner. It was simply a need to be addressed, a scratch to be itched.

Speaking of itches, "You know what pisses me off more than anything?" Tyce remarked directly after his fourth encounter that first week in the dorms. I was betting it wasn't widespread poverty or human-rights violations. "Getting an itch right before coming. You're pumping away, and five seconds before the gusher you get this little itch on your leg. You quickly scratch the thing knowing you've got all of four seconds to solve it, but there's still a trace of it left. And the little bastard steals the whole show from your orgasm." This was Tyce's version of a bad day.

Tyce regularly juggled a desire for kicks and an intent to honor the values of his conservative upbringing. He seemed to forever have the proverbial angels and devils trailing him, and paid heed to whichever was more convincing at the moment. Tyce, a true gentleman, never initiated anything too controversial, but if someone he respected launched such a thing, he'd not only partake but would carry it to an interesting extreme.

An example: Tyce initially tiptoed around the issue of pot smoking—I just assumed he never indulged—until Don offhandedly produced a joint one morning. "Got a match to go with that?" was Tyce's response. The pressing responsibilities of the day that included meeting with his advisor, buying books and attending class left him undeterred. In fact, Tyce reasoned that successfully completing these affairs stoned would provide a strong sense of accomplishment. An unstoned appointment with an advisor is tedious and uneventful; a post-joint meeting includes the challenge of focusing on what the lady is saying as opposed to the buzzing of the air conditioner, constructing a coherent block of statements in response, then actually remembering what the hell was just discussed. With the help of Visine, lots of practice and blind faith the mind won't disintegrate to a base level, it can be done. But from strictly a physical level, you just wouldn't think Tyce would be the one doing it, especially with such eventual frequency.

But a good thing came out of all this: Tyce's newfound curiosity with mystical consciousnesses also dispatched him to the land of excellent music. For the principal advantage any stoned mind has over the unstoned one is that the difference between good and bad music becomes obvious in a flash. Tyce, high as bird, pieced the revelation together in a matter of weeks. No greater treasure could be drifted upon by anyone.

8

The construction of Westfall Hall was perplexing. Its designers apparently used the same blueprint for the dorm as they would for any other apartment building. Very few signs of college proofing were evident anywhere. The project, surely in an effort to cut costs, had an illogical bent to it. And it bit the university in its large ass in the long run.

I mean, some things just begged to be abused. Like the elevator, for instance. It took all of 20 seconds to halt the lift between floors, pry the doors open, and hop on the top of the box. But this type of riding, however unconventional, got old and fast. You'd leap up there, feeling as giddy as if you broke the law or something, then would realize elevator surfing is nearly as boring as going up and down *in* the fuckin' thing. Through trial and error, we discovered the experience became livelier when discreetly harassing the oblivious passengers below. Had a video game or VCR been up there to occupy us, things might have been different.

Rusty had a cool trick designed to drive certain female riders bats. He'd only use it on passengers he knew. It was a tedious, painstaking process. He'd start with a whisper of the chick's name at a volume even

I perched *next* to him could barely hear. He'd sound it off again and again, each time cranking the volume up exactly one decibel. It was plain when it finally registered with the innocent rider below. A dog cocks its head in such situations, whereas a human tends to swivel it on the neck 10 or 12 degrees while assembling a faraway, perplexed look. They're both acts of acknowledging sound—a physical response to a sensory perception. Except Rusty was so adept at this, still another possibility surfaced—that the rider was also going completely bonkers from the voices in her head.

Don liked to spark a bowl on the roof of the unit on these occasions, directing silent billows of smoke down into the elevator transporting some studious, dedicated student towards the lobby. It would leave the crowd awaiting the lift wondering why the stoner on board couldn't just burn one in his room with a towel under the door like everyone else.

Not all elevator high jinks were subtle. With a bladder heavy from too many light beers, Renny at times had little choice but to spring a leak through the holey plastic ceiling into the elevator itself, though never directly on the rider. He had the good manners to arc the spout where the dude wasn't. It was probably assumed to be some kind of plumbing error. I repeat though, he never once doused a rider to my knowledge. Renny may have had the first impulse of a barbarian, but he had the soul of a gentleman. This proved it.

Physical dorm defects abounded. The ceilings weren't high at all, and consisted of that paperboard shit inviting every drunk 5-foot-10 and over to leap and punch them in. They were so low, you were tempted to smack them *sober*, just for spite. The floors had cheap carpeting with a thick padding underneath which housed all present and historical vomitings. This ensured a puke-aroma would waft through the wing at all times. The dorm administrators did little about it, and purposely I imagine. They'd send someone to tidy up the mess with a solution that looked suspiciously like H2O. It's not like they didn't get back at us for all of this.

The walls were paper-thin. They made your stereo seem even mightier than it was. The stairs were all wrong. Stairs are primarily used for smuggling ugly persons of the opposite sex out of the building in the morning to correct a drunken miscue the night before; their design is such that it's impossible for a fellow stair-taker to prove that the troll clomping behind you is actually with you. They're a pretty sharp invention. The Westfall stairs however spilled into a well-trafficked area by the lobby, canceling all effectiveness. They made not a lick of sense. In fact little *did* make sense about the entire dorm's design.

The beds weren't singles, they were halves. Tall sorts were provided mattress to around the knee area, then were on their own. They were difficult enough to sleep on solo, much less with a woman. They were strictly missionary-position beds. In fact they were so narrow, you and your date had to even *sleep* in the missionary position.

The toilet paper was about as effective as wax paper. It didn't actually remove any shit from the ass, it just displaced it. It took the layer of crap on the asshole and thinned and widened it, that's all.

So in this unholy dwelling, the rooms were too crowded, the air stunk, the ceilings were low, the walls and beds were too thin and too narrow, the toilet paper wasn't absorbent enough, the carpet was *too* absorbent, and the stairs emptied in a ridiculous location. And, of course, such was the perfect residence for all the rejects of west 11.

9

It didn't take long for Tyce and Wilt to rise to the ranks of top-notch AOP material. Eventually, they helped shape AOP as much as anyone. Both were canny bottle tippers. The pair possessed the prerequisite looks and charm. And, most importantly, each proved to be masters at picking up women. Their modi operandi usually employed wacky tactics for this end, but polar degrees of wackdom, if that makes sense. I luckily could adapt to both styles of meeting women. Wilt and Tyce's methods however, when employed in tandem, at times were ineffective. It seems in the multi-layered world of wackiness, some gray areas lack consensus concerning direction.

Both Wilt and Tyce when drunk have confidences and successes around women that may be unparalleled. Wilt's dorm methods relied on creating environmental opportunity. Some prop or excuse was created to initiate conversation; we'd spend all of three seconds thinking something up. Our first month in Westfall lacked creativity, banging on any old chick's door: "Is Linda in? She doesn't? Well what's your name…" It was a stale method that was surprisingly effective due to its timing—being all strangers, women welcomed any excuse to make acquaintances. Our plan was to strike early, before the insecure ones could mobilize peer groups to wall out those of our ilk. The system would only bomb when an ill-timed pizza was simultaneously delivered to the targeted room. Oh, the collective agony of the women inside! They sure couldn't chomp on that fattening shit in front of you. Nor could they offer you a piece, because delivered pizza kicks in a greed factor that's unrivaled. It strangely exists in all of us. So the pie just sits there, like it was ordered for the aromatic scent alone. Tension and pepperoni fill the air. But our initial visits, eventually to every even-floored room in the dorm, with bottle in hand leading the way, delivered a powerful message to our sweet neighbors what was in store for the school year.

By October, a six-floor mass opinion regarding our methods was brewing, and before any councils could convene and decisions mandated we switched operations to the neighboring dorms. And we became more creative in our efforts. Once, while roaming the halls of Corbett, a dorm with even finer women than the ones in Westfall, Wilt and I ventured into a storeroom, emerging with a broom. What a fine prop was had for the day! We became door-to-door broom salesmen with gusto. We pointed out all the amazing uses for a broom—as an air guitar, as a percussion device to get the upstairs neighbor to stop humping so loudly, as a way of waking up your roommate by jamming the bristles in her face, etc. One girl actually took us up on buying it, throwing us for a loop—we stammered that actual final sales required our manager's stamp of approval. Whatever that meant.

How to describe Wilt's demeanor in these situations? It's close to a stream-of-consciousness method, usually relying on some physical stimulus in front of him to kick off the conversation. He'd pick up on an item like the chick's fine stomach (say she was wearing a half shirt). He'd devote three sentences to the stomach at hand, then reach into general philosophies on stomachs in general (it's oddly his favorite feature). He'd compare and contrast the prevailing stomach with stomachs he'd known in the past, and with fantasy stomachs. Eventually, he'd have the woman accepting that her stomach, filtered through the impossible standard of a stomach expert, not only held its own but rode in front of the stomach pack. It's seduction in its subtlest manner—the form of unique flattery. And when blended with a dash of off-the-wall commentary to spice things up, it worked extraordinarily well.

Tyce operated on a more complex level. And around friends and strangers alike, he became increasingly enigmatic. I believe it was directly correlated to his accelerated pot intake. Around a newly met female acquaintance, Tyce was purposefully esoteric, in strict defiance of his cowboy look. Sure, he had the dialect and a host of western mannerisms, but they were often linked with comment and observation directly from Mars. He was a combination of Roy Rogers and Timothy Leary. Yet none of this seemed to deter his successes, even with the most provincial girls. For the man overflowed with pick-up talent. Actually, with Tyce's looks he could have had the personality of a lamp, with okay results. Whatever archetype of a physical ideal Colorado women had, Tyce pretty much fulfilled. It most likely wouldn't have flown as well in California or New England; Tyce's nose for pussy, like a sixth sense, led him to the perfect latitudinal and longitudinal coordinates. And having an original personality that defied the look was just an added bonus.

Inexplicably, however, Tyce on rare occasion could be found shacked up with the hideous-looking girl. We at first couldn't figure if he was too wasted to discern, or if his libido simply would not accept the indignity of a weekend night spent without a woman. Actually, neither theory was correct. He had backup women a phone call away all over campus, so whiffing at the bars had no bearing on final outcomes. He simply chose to gamble with what was new and of little certainty—in true AOP fashion—even if he occasionally cursed and kicked himself the following morn.

10

AOP friendships differ from other friendships in life because they're essentially a means by which to solve the mysteries of the world through *self*-discovery. So in fact they're a vessel, a complement to the immense learning process in college. For your best friend on a Friday night is truly the woman you've just met. And a unique life force is synthesized upon connection, incapable of being replicated. The unexpectedness of the event, the nervous exchanges of music enjoyed and philosophies considered, and the subtle sexual tension that weaves each moment together create a singular experience. It's the peak of aliveness. After whatever energies conjure to bring complete strangers to rapid intimacy, it becomes evident that no greater, more uncommon friendship exists, no other to make you both as high for the moment. Conversation with the right women in these situations is nearly always gratifying and enlightening, once initial guards are dismantled. Most, unlike their male counterparts, are forever open to what's beyond their known experience, and are forever searching to sweetly enhance it. Their vision is unabashedly broad and romantic. They'll watch not with disdain but with funny curiosity as you disassemble all the things they were taught to hold dear. They can completely oppose what you're saying and for like reasons become madly attracted to you.

So the best AOPers are catalysts to such scenarios. They're environmental enhancers. On a Wednesday morning, Wilt and I would maybe exchange six words in an hour, if we were feeling talkative. When dining together, after 10 minutes I'd say, "Pass the salt"; he'd frown and reply, "You could have pointed." Yet that Friday night at a mad bash when life's essences were being sorted out, we'd finish each other's sentences. After shaking free of the mundane we became blood brothers. We needed a complement to thrive in vast AOP domains, which provided meanings and strange revelations, and were quite self-sufficient in the world of football scores and history papers. Our respect was summed in the fact that we never had one fight, one jealous moment over a chick, in hundreds of weekends. If we both had it for a girl, one of us would sportsmanly find another, or in fairness we might both make-out with the girl, letting her decide. In paired-woman situations, one of us would end up with the less-attractive woman exactly half the time. Some biosocial equilibrium was clearly at work.

These weekend nights were the only times Wilt and I felt truly confident and self-assured in the world, and as a duo in these environs we began to feel indomitable. In school, Wilt and I never have taken efforts to prove our friendship. Its evidence is simply the fact that every time we hit the town, something out of the ordinary is gonna happen. Wilt in time became a magnet for some impaired, crazy or revelatory occurrence, generally with some impaired, crazy or revelatory women. Absolutely no one can break open life and get to the center as well as Wilt when he's partying. He'll howl in bitter objection at any bartender daring to bellow last call within earshot. Leaving a party never occurs to him without reminders, even if the sun is sneaking towards the sky. Sometimes the host herself has to escort him to the street after everyone else is long gone and point the grinning madman home. Wilt in time developed the purest understanding of what the Art of Partying is all about. He's a *Sensei* AOPer. But his was an AOP friendship, thus one of unconventionality, i.e. flourishing while acquiring other relationships.

Interestingly, women's friendships are often diametrically opposite. They'll feed each other's attentions endlessly, buying each other candles and stuffed animals and checking in with calls at work and shit, then will stab each other mercilessly in the back when the first zit-faced frat boy flashes his braces. It's bizarre. These sweet, fascinating creatures flaunt a barbed soul when dealing with their own kind. And Christ, they're the ones who deserve that crap the least.

11

Some time around mid-semester I met Cyndi—a beautiful, uncommon woman with whom I became somewhat attached. AOP relationships often skirt the ordinary, and my and Cyndi's was no exception. Cyndi was a fiercely independent woman, so fully secure with herself that she created her own rules for living. And on top of all that, she was gorgeous, with a set of breasts nearly indescribable. I'm going to try here, but trust me—it won't do them justice.

Her breasts were two perfectly sculpted works of art. They were big—damn big—jugs easily noticeable behind an extra-large flannel shirt. These on a small, thin frame. They were as full as melons—*water*melons—loaded with width, height and depth, with a small army of subcutaneous muscles working overtime to support them. When breasts are this inflated, they generally have little choice but to assume a generic roundness—either somewhat firm/round or droopy/pendulous-round. Cyndi's, however, despite their enormity, were packed with shape to make any *little* tit envious. They were blessed with the coveted ski-jump contour that originated at the pectoral muscle, sloped down, and then somehow outward, raising the nipples. It was as if God himself had attached a fine fish wire to her nipples—the pervert—and levitated them towards the heavens. Indeed, the classic ski-jump form eludes most small tits; discovering it on bigguns makes for a rare treasure.

Her areolas were situated high on the breast, occupying a moderate 10 percent of surface space, even when unstimulated. Immense, amorphous areolas taking up half of a huge breast I personally find frightening. That's as large as your face. Areolas, for those down on terminology, are the extra-pigmented launching pads for the nipples. Ideally, the nipple is located around the middle of the areola. If it's above or below the areola or off to the side, something is very wrong. The areola by nature is a bit wrinkled and relatively dark in color. This is because all the erecting and de-recting of the nips for years and years takes a toll on the neighboring tissue. It becomes weathered. A thin body bearing a small areola placed high on a big breast with a well-centered, erect nipple is pretty much an ideal. And yes, such properties adorned Cyndi.

Perhaps the only fatal flaw of the huge shapely breast on a college coed is the possible lack of a proper nipple erection. Sadly, the large breast, in all its glory, simply cannot compete with the small-breasted nipple erection. In fact, the smaller the tit, the bigger and more resolute the nipple erection. It's the ace up its sleeve. It's not uncommon for girls with pancakes for breasts to boast inch-and-a-half posts as compensation. One could very nearly play a game of horseshoes on them. The nipples alone struggle to atone for the sea level elevation. Most bigguns exhibit adequate nipple erections, but I've been around a few incapable of being stimulated. They were seven-inch tits mis-equipped with a stock three-inch nerve root. It rendered them impotent. Cyndi's nips of course, sitting high and gorgeous, had no such downfall.

Her breasts were double bouncers. Any slight variance of the body's vertical position elicited an instant one-two bounce from the tits. Any pace beyond a mild stroll did it. Sitting and standing of course did it. Stairs did it to such a degree that a specific synchronization was required to safely climb them. They were so perfectly formed, no six-pound brasserie was needed to shape them. Relatively free to explore the thoracic area, they did so, and with abandon.

It's very, very difficult to concentrate on much at all when a woman with large, ski-jumped, double bouncers is before you. I personally get sweaty palms. Plus, the body manufactures extra adrenaline that makes you shake when it's about that time to make it with her. I swear if I'm engaged with such a woman I've gotta first hit the can and do 40 silent pushups in the cramped quarters to burn off all the shake energy. The power and allure of the large breast in a form-fitting shirt is not easily explained. The things easily dominate the room; sometimes the entire building. Not 14 seconds of intense philosophical discourse with the woman can pass without the mind continually harking back to the more pressing issue of the breasts.

Cyndi was surely aware of all this. Yet she was also mindful she was far beyond just a physical specimen, so a minor competition existed between her and her own tits. The three parties vied for attentions and were equally persuasive. To assert the upper hand, she'd often wear a big baggy shirt or sweater, in attempts to divert the focus off her tits and up to the words exiting her mouth. This only worked partially, for it took a shirt like a pup tent to completely neutralize their presence.

But truly, behind the amazing breasts was an amazing woman. Cyndi was a talented artist, and was especially gifted at pencil sketching. She had a photographic memory—I'd give her a page from a book to read once; she'd close her eyes, pause a second, then recite it verbatim. The perfect joy for me was reading in my room, then hearing Cyndi's unmistakable gentle knock on my door. I'd be greeted by this gorgeous, unique creature standing there with a shy smile. "Hey," is what she'd say. She'd usually break out a joint, and gradually our reticent selves would drift toward some odd subject that only pot can track down.

Cyndi was so self-sufficient she was a near loner. She had few female friends. Living a life this way, especially for a woman, invites social strain; to compensate, these sorts often adopt a brashness or stock defensiveness to fend off the accompanying bleats from the herd. This wasn't at all evident in Cyndi. Contrarily, she was more apt to say nothing to people she found either insulting or uninteresting. Or to people she liked for that matter, for she was the rare woman who felt no obligation to fill conversational gaps with idle chatter. Silent air in the midst of her and someone else created no discomforts. So when she did talk, since the creation of words was to convey an idea rather than nervously patch dead-air holes, it was usually worth hearing. Her voice was confident yet contained a soft vulnerability, a sweet indefiniteness about it. She was exceedingly smart, but always allowed for the fallibility of opinion—closing nothing off—respecting the vast potential of idea.

Cyndi screwed with frequency, and with exactly whomever she wanted. Yet her sexual encounters never extended beyond the physical. She interestingly banged lots of shallow jock types, whose minds she (perhaps purposely) had little in common with. She made certain the sex could never lure her into a relationship. Sex and commitment not only were incompatible for Cyndi, they were polar elements. Hell, she could have taught hard-core AOPers a thing or two.

Which leads me to my forlorn situation. Cyndi banged Tyce, she screwed Wilt, both of whom she regarded with indifference. But since she had great feelings for me, I was deemed off limits. What kind of fucked-up justice is that?? True, at times we'd get drunk and I'd obsessively play with her famous breasts, and kiss her soft, excellent mouth. But come 3 a.m. following a party, or after I was diligently cramming for a mid term with Cyndi faithfully providing moral support, at bedtime she'd rather conspicuously make a little pillowed spot on the floor for herself. And lying in bed, I'd watch this strange, beautiful creature curl up like a cat and doze off, one bitten fingernail forever beyond my reach.

12

Once, and only once, Tyce attempted to bring a respectable date to the west "U" on 11. It was by severe accident. He somehow thought he could graze the cyclone without getting sucked in. The miscue ambushed an otherwise honorably intended evening with his date Mary, a knockout sorority girl from Denver. Tyce had made plans for the two to dine at an upscale restaurant, take in a good movie comedy, then catch a nightcap at a classy lounge; they made it exactly 1/3 of the way. The date started as a charming, sparkling, moonlit stroll with a cultured, well-mannered and stunning woman; it concluded as a darkened, swirl-cloud spin in a tequila typhoon. Tyce by now regularly roiled in the eye of the AOP hurricane, yet, true to his diametric self, still maintained distinct ties to calm, fair-weathered sailing. Especially if it meant angling for gorgeous women. In these situations he'd shamelessly revert to clean-cut valedictorian in a snap. His chameleon-like demeanor was ever determined by the whimsical weather vane that was his dick. Sadly, however, when Tyce's righteous alter ego *did* emerge, it was greeted with stubborn, highly unaccommodating surroundings.

A friend of Tyce's from Denver set up the distant introduction. Mary and Tyce took interest in each other's pictures; the two had a few phone conversations, then agreed to meet the upcoming Saturday night. Mary had won a number of beauty pageants and had the wholesome, all-American personality such contests require. Tyce was gushing nervously all week. He kept repeating, "Something feels right about this girl," a line that drove us nuts by Wednesday. He only knew her by photographs and phone conversations, but developed a keen respect and admiration for Mary, which actually spilled into his non-Maryed life. In fact the words "slammed," "boffed," "porked," "injected," and "speared" conspicuously disappeared from his vocabulary, at least for the one week.

The new G-rated Tyce chivalrously picked Mary up in Denver and brought her back to town. After a too-expensive dinner and a fine bottle of wine at a restaurant in the foothills, Tyce's cash level descended to the single digits. And, luck had it, he absentmindedly left his ATM card in the dorm room. It created a huge predicament. He was against exposing this fine, delicate creature to what might be on west 11, yet knew it was absurd to have the gem wait for him in the dorm's dark parking lot. He just had to gamble that everyone on the floor was out partying somewhere else.

Tyce was decked in a suit. I think it was his prom garb or something. Mary was clad in a frilly, white dress. She had a fresh flower in her hair. They boarded the elevator and pressed "11." Before the lift reached the fifth floor, Tyce smelled trouble. He registered a faint drumbeat and guitar sound, which became exponentially louder with each passing floor. As the doors parted on 11, a Nirvana tune was blasting so loudly, the elevator shook in noticeable palpitations. "Come…as you are…as you were…as I want you to be…" the song lectured Tyce. Andre was passed out directly in front of the elevator doors, in what looked to be an unsuccessful escape attempt. His eyes were the proverbial two X's. Before Mary could comment Tyce stammered, "He'll be all right—poor fellah was up all last night studying." Tyce was as tense as a guitar string now, knowing all the work invested in his good behavior could in a flash be reduced to guano. He bent to tie his shoes, stalling for time to sort things. Mary sensed his nervousness. "Anything wrong?" she pleasantly bellowed over the music. Tyce felt pangs of paternal protectiveness, a need to battle all evils and wrongs in her sweet, small universe. He shoved the hall door to the west "U" forward, grabbed Mary's hand and attempted a beeline for the ATM card.

It was as if the event triggered an action sequence in a Bruce Lee movie. "Hiiiiyaahhhhhh!" Renny howled maniacally, four feet off the ground, in full karate kick. The crash of fire extinguisher glass sounded like a misplaced cymbal amid the blaring music. Glass shards segregated in all directions, some resting within a foot of Mary's flitting dress. Tyce and Mary stood in frozen wonder. Renny was scary drunk and bouncing everywhere; Darrell, Rusty and Gerry were dancing wildly in the hall, scream/singing made-up words against the made-up ones of Cobain's. Wilt and I straddled the doorway of my room making friends with some girls from the floor above. Wilt slow-motionedly balanced a too-full shot towards his face then belted it down chaserless, cringing. Nearly every damned door to every room was open, each contributing a piece of music or madness to the mayhem. Kile, the mother hen of the floor, found a broom amid the chaos and busily swept the glass in a pile, out of harm's way. Don was surveying the scene with contained amusement from a corner, smoking a joint solo.

Renny spotted Tyce, double taking. "Tyce you motherfucker! You mother- fucking fucker! You fucking fucker! Get over here and do a shot!!" The well-dressed lass aside him was invisible to the drunken maniac. Tyce wilted three full inches. He turned and looked behind him, with meager hopes of finding a no-good drunk also named Tyce. Mary examined this new incarnation up and down. Tyce's cover was in pieces, like the fire extinguisher glass. He began to shake right where he stood. All reddened eyes on the floor curiously watched, as some violent transformation in the guy seemed to be occurring. Would he strike Renny down and hover over him, proving his intolerance for this kind of behavior? Would he then valiantly heave Mary over his shoulder and carry her down the stairs, far from this place of sin to the land of properness, never to be seen again?

It was not to be. It in fact turned out to be a sad day for decency. Tyce, you see, could only witness so much debauchery before he felt obligated to help shape its outcome. He released Mary's hand, slowly walked towards a large bottle of tequila, and sloshed full a shot glass. He asked Mary if she wouldn't mind, then, in a solo toast, slammed it down before she could answer. The act was repeated three or four times. It was like the wolf man versus the full moon. Old Tyce was never really short of good intentions; he just had trouble fulfilling them to their required ends.

But to everyone's surprise, especially Tyce's, Mary wasn't such an unspoiled Susie after all. In fact she kicked back a couple shots herself. She and Tyce had their similarities all right: clean-cut, attractive exteriors concealing kicks-laden souls. It just took the right situation to help Mary shed her skin. The two took a couple minutes to reintroduce themselves, then Tyce scrambled again for the tequila, the limes and the salt, shoveled them in a corner of the room and, elbows wide, began digging in. He looked like a pack dog defending his dinner. You got the sense if you wandered too near the shot glass he'd bite you. Apparently he was just designing ways to offset our huge head start. Now in his own element, he spoke in assured tones with Mary between shots.

"Awright, listen and listen good. See the big crazy sumbitch there who just who tried to set the fire extinguisher free? Never, *never* respond to any mentionings of a family feud." Tyce too had been snookered by Renny, despite my warnings. In fact everybody on the floor was eventually burned, and it became routine to dole a quick tutoring to newcomers. "Be careful." he again warned. "He's tricky."

And he was. But now with the essentials behind them they could get to partying. Tyce put down two more quick shots; Mary mirrored it as daintily as one can. Speaking of mirrors, some idiot broke open a bunch of black-beauty study capsules on one; Mary and company were actually snorting the shit. The girl was nearly ruling the fuckin' party! The white powder was sprinkled with strange black seeds, with the shit burning the nasal cavity like strychnine. Renny's nose started to bleed—he delighted himself with the macabre effect, and did little to correct it. He sought more glass to smash, and wandered off.

Rusty stumbled in, filling the void. "Who's got the stuporifity, the general ballishness and incapable resolutions to kindly join me for a shot?" he clearly inquired. He was carrying his own private supply. No one took him up on it, for Rusty was a heaver, and an uncontrolled one, which is the worst kind. He could be dancing and jamming full tilt to a song and suddenly, spontaneously—"wreuhhhh"—redesigning a patch of wallpaper in the room. You always found yourself subconsciously corralling him away from the stereo system, the CDs, and the girl you were interested in.

Out of the blue, and in blue, a campus cop crashed the party. And his appearance struck at perhaps the most inopportune time imaginable, as the speakers blasted "One Way Out," by the Allman Brothers. Surely, anyone with the sense of a mule knows nothing in life can warrant interrupting that perfect song. Rusty and I were entranced into the screaming solo—he air-guitaring the Dickey Betts part and I wailing on slide, with all eyes tightly shut in unwavering concentrations.

Suddenly, a large, penetrating voice went "Hey!" The guitar went out of tune; the drum set toppled over. Who would rudely "Hey!" through "One Way Out"?? we wondered, as the song crumbled to pieces. We knew it couldn't have been a west elevenite. We may have collectively been debased, depraved and degenerated, but heaven knows we were never impolite. The solo was in tatters, the tune unsalvageable. We could've spun it again, but it wouldn't have had the same punch. All these thoughts occurred in 1/10 of a second. We opened our eyes to examine the foul soul who stole our sacred song from us. It was a cop; an uninvited one no less.

He was excited he finally had our undivided attentions. "TURN DOWN THE GODDAMNED MUSIC NOW!! TURN THE GOD-DAMNED MUSIC DOWN NOW!!" He pointed his finger at the stereo, so we could locate it. Now, different factors came into play here. I, like most folks, normally would have unthinkingly followed the order, if for no other reason than the source was wearing a ridiculous looking uniform. It's just pathetic instinct. And then, realizing I blindly obeyed a rude, disrespectful piece of stool who entered *my* hall and *my* room, shouting orders at *me*, I would have dealt him a rash of shit. That didn't happen.

Might've happened during Joan Osborne's "Ladder." Or a U2 tune or Santana's version of "She's Not There." But the poor fellow had the bungled timing to test his machismo during (other than Joe Cocker's "The Letter") the greatest live song ever recorded. Now, in the split second of thought involved I did rationalize that out of all segments of society, the one with the piss-poorest musical taste could very well be the cop faction. So there *was* a moderate chance this ignoramus was simply oblivious of the etiquette attached to "One Way Out." But this barking business hit a sore nerve. See, these guys belong to this whole barking hierarchy, like the military, whereas their superiors bark at them and they bark at the rookies who then go home and bark at their dogs or their wives (who are often one and the same). I'm personally light years from this funny ritual, doing little barking of my own and thus expecting exactly no barking from others in return, no matter *who* the fuck they are. So in *my* home, all this was strictly out of context.

So I closed the door and locked it. Now technically speaking, the cop's order was honored, since the heavy wooden door now separating the cop and the music served as an excellent sound muffler. But somehow he didn't see it that way. In fact he began clubbing on the door, proving he wasn't all that serious about silencing the joint after all. We tried the heralded song again. "Buh badah la buh buh ba ba ba, Buh badah la buh…"

It sounded like the cop was trying to percuss with it, way out of time, and was ruining it yet again. I don't mind a lack of rhythm if the heart is in it, but this was a farce. Rusty initially found the whole situation hilarious, but became nervous about the time the singing kicked in, when everything finally registered in his slow moving, wasted brain. The bastard wasn't even plucking on his tennis racket anymore.

"We gotta open it man—they'll bust it down," Rusty pleaded in surrender. That I'd have liked to see. Dorm doors weigh about 2000 pounds apiece; when they slam from the wind they're heard for miles. It'd take that wimpy campus cop, six rookie recruits and a junior detective to batter *this* sucker down. It appeared however that the song was unredeemable—a felony offense on the cop's part—so I relented.

"Pah ya (inaudible shriek) bah bat!" he yelled.

"Pardon me?" I politely bellowed back. He sounded like a pre-pubescent kid who just placed all his marbles in his mouth. Then Rusty hit the power button on the stereo, kicking in another realm.

This time his words exited sharply, unambiguously. "Put your hands behind your back!" Without the music a cold, vulnerable reality set in, sapping me of my super- human strength. I had no choice but to try and negotiate.

"Hey, I was just playing around," I reasoned with the cop. Showing a lack of an offbeat sense of humor, he cuffed me, just where he ordered the hands, and marched me to the car. It probably gave the bastard a hard-on.

13

I think people would be able to find contentment if they just had a good dose of understanding in the world. To offer whatever version they choose to portray of themselves and have it received correctly by others. That didn't happen in this case. Now I had no problem with the facts of the situation, with the cop and all. In fact I was kind of proud of them, in a twisted way. But it turned out the campus cops were investigating a table that was hurled out of an eleventh-floor-lobby window that night, and when I was arrested and hauled to the paddy wagon, the gobs of onlookers assumed *I* was the table tosser. This made me feel like some drunken jerk with no respect for law and order. Christ, if folks departed the dorm the same moment the table was heaved, they would have met their maker. So my perception amongst some dormites was upgraded from rebellious wag to potential ruthless killer in just under an hour. I hate to brag, but that's a helluva promotion!

Events as these are meant to trigger the societal learning process. When a college student makes a conscious choice to get his kicks challenging the law, he pays fines, spends nights in jail, and eventually decides it ain't fun anymore. It starts out great, but the payoff gets to be not worth the investment. The societal directive here is not unlike the breaking of a horse. The horse eventually does what he's supposed to do to avoid any further beatings.

Unfortunately, while unruly behavior often faces discipline, non descript or dull behavior generally gets off without a hitch. No one gets hauled off in the back of a squad car sitting sideways on cuffed wrists for watching too many sit coms. They sure as fuck *should*, but they don't. So over time, people become conditioned to behave not badly and/or dully. This is why dullness increases proportionately with age.

So I imagined after my court date I'd learn numerous lessons and would embark on the somber journey towards dulldom. And 10 years down the line I'd be driving around with a MADD bumper sticker and collecting door-to-door for the police fund. But, miraculously, Judge Smoltz saved me. I opted to plead not guilty to the charge of "interference," and the old judge who died months later of a heart attack (I hope unrelatedly) somehow sided with me. I was brutally honest, remarking that my disrespect was only a reflection of the cop's, etc., but truly didn't expect this cog in the wheel to reward such a defense. After all, assholishness accompanies most cops' territory. Anyone dubbed with politeness, diplomacy and erudition sure as hell wouldn't pick law enforcement as a career.

But it only sets you up for the big fall. Months later, during a huge street party, I was busted for the same charge by cops trying to clear out a party. I legitimately was looking for my ride, and was spotted by two cops who had ordered me to leave 20 minutes earlier. The cops didn't buy the flimsy excuse that it's difficult to leave a party when you can't find the folks who gave you a ride. They too attended the military school of reasoning: you get an order, you follow it, even if you have to hoof it 10 miles home. Upon arrest I was so astounded, I couldn't even properly assemble myself into an asshole, at least initially. Now this situation *was* incontrovertible abuse of power by the oinkers. So, being not an illogical sort, I figured since I prevailed in the first case, and since we are blessed with a relatively uniform and fair judicial system, I'd win this case and any like successive ones. My victory proved my leash of issue was a long one, allowing ample area to frolic about in the world. So come court time, I bounded in like I owned the place. The cop approached beforehand and offered a deferred sentence in lieu of the trial. I brushed him aside. He's running, I figured. After I said my piece to the judge, he considered it for three full seconds, found me guilty, and smashed a roach with his gavel. It was a deliverance of the cold, hard knock of reality.

14

I was lying on the couch in our suite one afternoon, recovering from a long Friday night, when Kile concocted a reason to interrupt me. Kile was the white sheep of the gang on west 11. He was erudite, conservative, career oriented and other frightening adjectives. To AOP, Kile was the foil incarnate. He'd attempt all sorts of methods to get AOPers to redirect their lives toward a more sensible, reasonable reality. Kile interestingly was never wholly repulsed by AOPers like our ex-roommie Colin, he simply felt it was his life-calling to reform them. And he worked with an evangelical zeal.

Kile enjoyed approaching me in circumstances like these, since I'm fairly inarticulate when I'm hungover. So, even though he was a common fool, he'd often emerge from our debates seemingly victorious.

On this occasion, Kile bit straight into the meat 'n' potatoes of AOP: sex. Perhaps unnerved that he hadn't been laid in a long time, maybe *ever*, he was working overtime to convince himself of the pitfalls of such behavior. Kile's opinions naturally always made practical sense, at least surfacely. But I never understood why the guy supported them with such adamancy, or even bothered with them at all. I mean if I somehow maintain a stock point of view on a subject, I sure as hell ain't gonna flaunt it all over the place. It's embarrassing enough *un*spoken. How the guy could so passionately defend the status quo, I find an amazing mystery.

Kile started hurling the spears from the get go. "You guys are pathetic. You masochists party like maniacs so you hate yourselves the next day, then justify it by assigning some kind of religious significance to the mess. You spray the fire extinguisher at people and under their doors in total idiocy, and pretend it's some kind of baptism. I think it's all out of fear. Fear you yourself are the ordinary person you despise, fear of a real commitment to the opposite sex, fear of graduation, fear of getting a responsible job."

He had a large whitehead on his forehead, inducing still another fear, that it would spontaneously bust in my room.

"You clowns are always talking about fulfillment," he continued. "Fulfillment isn't short term, and it's not temporary. That's a contradiction. Anyone can get immediate gratification from a slimy one-night stand. You want a real challenge? Try tendering a *long*-term relationship. See what it takes to make *that* work."

I rewinded a few sentences. Anyone, eh? Stick a pair of eyelashes on that zit and the fucker could make money as a Halloween costume.

"The world is operating way too fast for such nonsense, Kile m' boy," I guessed. "You talk like an old man with too few choices. We're sitting on the one moment in life when the usual can be dropkicked for a short time. You've got your entire post-college life to behave like an old biddy. What's the rush?"

And his choices *were* limited, by my calculations. It wasn't staunch discipline keeping the books open on a Saturday night so much as it was a prescription of his physical makeup. But I had to put it to the guy gently.

"The same voice telling AOP to go in the other direction, warns you to stick to the beaten path," I said. "Each human characteristic, every personality trait seals off a good chunk of our fate. You're simply genetically built to study on Saturday nights. But I also believe even the yous in the world have some pre-death need somewhere to raise some hell. To bend the rules forth a good tug, then snap 'em back, in some prig's face. And what better time than college to exercise that demon from the soul? I fear that young, stoic sorts as yourself are destined to crack somewhere down the line, cheating on their wives or becoming cocaine heads at 45, just trying to complete themselves."

Actually I wasn't nearly as eloquent as all that. I spat out the gist of the above, then silently cursed myself for the mess coming out sideways, like an ass-first-birth baby. I can't talk when I'm hungover and he knew it.

Kile *was* eloquent, but one-dimensionally, like a lawyer. "You illustrate precisely why one should resist such temptations. If we *are* bored creatures, with inbred capabilities of going off the deep end, forays into this AOP stuff will only create bigger appetites. My suggestion is to keep Pandora's box as tightly closed as possible for as long as possible." The double-entendre surely eluded him.

Restraint. Discipline. Order. How'd he ever survive on the "U," I wondered? The clown was a poster boy for the Marines.

A last worder like myself chose to let it go. Who was I to even *want* to change him? People like Kile not only keep the machine well lubed, but also provide the perfect counter to AOP. Subtract everyone like Kile from the formula, and we'd *all* be Kiles. AOP, PTA— there'd be no difference. It's just a matter of relativity.

So maybe AOP is not much more than a good shove against these inanimate souls. A part of me (as well as Kile) thinks it's as shallow as that. But the other half thinks it goes beyond that, seeking some greater purpose or change, attempting to spread the college gospel of frivolous joy and strange enlightenment throughout one's self and others. What more noble way to pay homage to these sacred stomping grounds? But these are weird times. Serene, untroubled, business-like times. It's enough to make you pine for any old twisted ideal of campus past. Or to make you take a fist to the fire-extinguisher glass.

College used to be (at least in my romanticized image) fertile terrain for foolish idealisms and wayward directions, a muse for some slanted, wounded vision warring with those mired in the plurality. And it wasn't until after graduation, when the vision fizzled with futility, that it was finally surrendered to the other side. But times have changed. Students now sign up with the goddamned majority right off the bat without even *messing* with the futile dream. It's enough to make you want to take your fist to the fire- extinguisher glass.

It's not hard to see why the futility gap has been widened to the point of not even trying—why folks en masse are choosing the unblinking path of college, career, family and IRAs in some fucked-up order. For recent history provides a daunting model. I mean, look at the half million at the original Woodstock. All of these "revolutionaries" are now magically dispersed in suburbia, with such perfect markings and blendings it's impossible to tell who's who at the community pool. And the fact that these very clowns are at the helm of a culture in possibly its most vacuous, law-filled, complacent state ever, makes a pretty poor advertisement for the lasting integrity of the "visionary."

It goes to show that the self-preservation powers of society's core—all that's reasonably good, that which is purely fucked, and the huge remainder perched in the middle of the road, waiting to be flattened by a truck—are miraculous. The 1960s provided the only formidable challenge the "system's" ever had—really just a small scuffle—and it rebounded more strongly and invincibly than ever. The beast learned lesson, gained insight, and has adjusted accordingly. Now most threats—any countercultural tendencies—are ingeniously diffused by assimilation. The most unifying musical calls to rebellion in the sixties are now backdrops to every third television commercial. Hard-core rappers telling it like it is quickly give up the fight and join the club with offerings of high-dollar movie contracts. Subversiveness, social deviance is in full remission. Traces occur, but innocuously, where the culture allows it to; yet it's nonexistent where it disturbs. The modern-day blue haired, makeup-wearing rock 'n' roller is as inoffensive as a baby in a stroller—he's just acting a rehearsed part. And such pandering makes a mockery of true rebellion and directed defiance. The populous has, in unsuspecting fashion, clawed its way backwards to being sleepy, obedient dupes. And the mighty hand of American society continues to mold the "free" mind the way it likes, always lending the impression it was its constituents' own will.

If not assimilated, the scant groups that do presently veer from the status quo are cannily discredited and discarded by the mainstream by virtue of their fringe element— anti-fur groups, feminist groups, environmental groups, even religious groups. Blandness has become the rallying cry of the streets. It could be that students face possibly the most docile, indifferent, piece-of-shit filled era in the country's short history. The Beats from the fifties and hipsters of the sixties are far removed what's from hip now, in fact they're caricatures, jokes on a sit com. Now hipness, impossibly, is in the mundane. It's found surfacely, pinned to the face of an empty, charismatic soul detached from an ideal. Taking an immoderate stand on anything, drifting too far left or right or up or down is what's uncool.

Thankfully, certain folks on west 11 showed some potential otherwise, but the general career-oriented mindset rampant on campus is mind-boggling. Half of these automatons don't even attempt a discernible variance from the mutual fund generation— their hair, clothes and attitudes nearly parallel mom and dad's.

It may be far-fetched to pin this perfusion of student apathy *on* old mom and dad. But maybe the blame can be split. Because it *is* apparent the great leaders of yesterday's counterculture who are now running things have ironically proven that any hopes of escaping the prefab ideal passed down from generation to generation are meager. All the boomers' railings of social injustice; ravings of a more meaningful, spiritual existence; implying of cultural revolution and preaching of self-liberation through hallucinogens are former ramblings of the same country-club fucks who now vote on the board to suspend college students for smoking a joint. These thick pieces of stool have, in full hypocrisy, piled up the crap the young, fresh-minded folk have to slog through today. They frolicked lavishly in a culture brimming with hopes of changing the world for the better; now, far removed from their prime, they've become staunch defenders of an even more regulated, inviolable order than the one they inherited 30 years back.

So, minus the illusory substance (and a few actual social upgrades), the 60s turned out to be not much more than one excellent party. Free love and mind expansion, mixed with a healthy dose of challenging the dogs of authority. The great gap of values wedged between generations only garnished the kicks. And campus was the epicenter of activity. It was a time when you could smoke a joint with your philosophy professor and link his lecture on existentialism with current events.

The real pisser is this generation can't even muster up *that*. We can't even party worth a fuck. These days your philosophy professor rats on you to the dean who commissions a drug test, resulting in a two-semester suspension. Alcohol-free fraternities are now the trend of a growing number of schools. Puritanism, 300 years later, has clambered its way back in vogue. So those who *do* party do it with abashment, guiltily, like they're violating a moral code. The night before they laughed harder than ever before, dangled from the twelfth floor ledge in the dorm and got laid to boot; the next morning they're flooded with the damnable remorse of actually having had a good time.

Give me a toilet-flush economy, with nary a job for a million graduates. Give me wars and starvation and oppressed souls realizing their plight, ready to take to the streets. Give me leaders so vile and mad that corruption hives manifest on their bodies. Take this abundance of collegiate zombies and shift the conveyer belt to reverse, far from this fine, doomed university. Give me the glory of shouting for the sake of shouting, the chance to peer through my one goddamned window of dis-opportunity. Let me wade like a pig in mud in the lie of the "dream." Give me a fuckin' life sentence for graduation, sell my empty soul to ol' Beelzebub himself, anything but four years of ordinariness in this hallowed, hollow institution.

Alas, as we students encounter this unruffled social fabric, this non-existent unifying bond valiantly detaching us from the dead-eyed majority, this lack of thread of discontent woven throughout the student bodies, it's apparent *something's* gotta be done. Hence, AOP. It's maybe a slice of the sixties mixed with a couple shots of present-day apathy. AOP certainly has no political agenda. It surely strives to make no long-term social impact on the world. But upon the stout seriousness of career direction and the vast proliferation of prudence, it wages a small, discreet war. These are the most dangerous of times, precisely because nobody knows it.

I covered all this in about six seconds of mind time, as Kile hovered over, poised for battle, awaiting a witty or pathetic rejoinder. I felt a certain pity for both of us losers. He wasn't the enemy, nor was I. Poor Kile anyway was from the classic "dysfunctional" family, giving him every reason to condemn the crap he dealt with while growing up. It's no coincidence such offspring are conspicuously devoid of AOP participation. In fact, in time AOP waged an informal research on the matter, with the results being as follows: If you regularly see your dad stumbling through the front door in a drunken stupor, smashing things, that's the last thing you're gonna want to do when you reach adulthood. It's those who experience healthy, loving upbringings who desire to get drunk and smash things in college. They just don't want to make a living out of it. The sad, dysfunctional folk stuff everything along these lines in a box with the label "addiction" plastered on it, and store it in the corner, out of sight. They caustically criticize AOPers throughout college for their irresponsibleness, and study diligently, albeit gloomily.

Later in life, when job pressures and divorce loom large, they begin to drink heavily, while smashing things. See, it's the timing that's way off.

15

At some point during the first semester, the fledgling college student begins to wonder the following: "Is this school right for me? Is it worth its tuition? Am I a good fit for this joint?" The personality of the school at this stage gets shouldered up to your own. Strong critical analyses are necessary here, examining all of the school's possible deficiencies. Usually, the most glaring cases are intelligence, kicks, personality and gorgeous women. If *all* these things are glaring, it's probably time to get some extra-dark shades and transfer the hell out of there.

> *Note: The following references to the "transfer meter" use a 1-to-100 scale.

- Lack of Intelligence

Graffiti pretty well indicates the IQ level of the school you've gotten yourself involved with. Check out the toilet stalls at the student union, or in various classroom halls. If the graffiti is intelligent, and sprinkled with literary allusions and witty, philosophical exchanges, that's a good sign. If the brunt of it is authored by queens who write "Good head here, 4:00" and latent queens who follow up with "Kill all Fags," you might be in for a long year. And no one's to blame but you and your pitiful high school scores. *Transfer-meter number for the Faulty Graffiti scenario: 88.

- Lack of Kicks

If no immediate kicks are to be found, sniff around for reasons why. Some institutions promote wholesomeness to near conspiratorial levels. They simply pulsate in prudence. Carefully examine campus-sanctioned material, like the student newspaper. Is every other editorial entitled something along the lines of: "College Drinking: Silent Killer?" Here's an easy one: Is the word "Christian" inserted somewhere in the name of the school? For example, did you accidentally matriculate at Tennessee *Christian* Military Academy University? This factor alone would indicate extremely poor nightlife, and day life as well. *Transfer-meter number for the Christian-in-the-Name oversight: 99.

- Lack of Personality

Sit in the student plaza, where the co-eds congregate. Do the environs foster creative self-expression, or do they seem to demand physical uniformity? Do all the hairstyles look like the same barber accomplished them? Does a large percentage of the student body provide free advertising for some clothes company? In the mean time, some of these conformities can be discreetly challenged. Wearing a Tommy Hilfucker shirt comes to mind. *Transfer-meter number for the Hilfiger syndrome: 101.

- Women With Perceived Physical Liabilities

I would say women or *men* with perceived physical liabilities, but women aren't so shallow they'd consider a transfer because campus was flooded with a bunch of homely, crewcutted men. However, if campus were flooded by reams of homely, crewcutted *women*, most guys would bolt, probably before Columbus Day. For the bolters, consider a simple piece of advice: Warm-weathered schools have better-bodied women. Cold weather breeds inactivity; also cellulite is too easily disguised with clothing. Long overcoats shroud mammoth rumps, down vests conceal rolled bellies, mufflers mask double chins, mittens obscure fattened fingers and ski hats veil engorged earlobes. This type of unreality can't dog warm-weathered schools.

The reason UT Austin, for example, has the largest student body in the country is because plump chicks do best by avoiding the place. The warm, sticky climate provides no easy way to disguise all the fat. Thin women who are wont to show off their wares jam the university, and the dudes follow in record numbers like puppies trailing their masters. *Transfer-meter number for the Crewcutted Fat-Women phenomenon: 92.

16

What compels me to act this way? There was a nice, well-groomed lad named Gerry, who, being Wilt's roommate, used to tag with us to parties and the like. Short kid with razor-straight blond hair who looked like he was in tenth grade. Gerry's strongpoint was his sense, unlike the rest of us, and armed with this carefully honed intuitive-type sense, he naturally refused to ride in my van. Even when I was *sober*. I'd say Gerry, I'm the best driver in the world, I just like to go fast, laddie, to add a bit of adventure to the tired old world on a routine dash to the market; but our friend, good sense and all, would politely defer. So it was a misty, drizzly evening when six of us rowdily piled into the van to attend a party about a mile away with Gerry deferring, opting to hoof it. I surveyed the evening sky, as the dark clouds muscled on in. Certainly a downpour was imminent. What staunch commitment, what unwavering values! All of us fools in the vehicle could have learned a lesson or two from this kid. We reverently waved to Gerry plodding along as the vehicle fishtailed sideways out of the slickened parking lot and on to the bash.

The party was sub-mediocre, and after two tedious hours we decided to head back to the dorms in hopes of finding something better. By this time a steady rain was coming down, and Gerry had no choice but to consider a lift. The group piled in, vying for a comfortable spot, then beckoned their friend. Gerry stood alone, with dampened hair glued to his head in a chaotic pattern. Either sweat or rain was dripping off his chin.

He peered in, neck outstretched, like one would into a lion's den. Friendly faces welcomed him, people he lived with, divvied up the phone bill with—what could be so horrible? They called to him gently, reassuringly. He examined the crew one by one: nary a rider had casted limb, none was worsened with rodded spine or mentally slowed from prior head injury. Nor was any evidence of trauma present from the first leg of the trip—the van seemed sound and all riders appeared healthy and with able judgment. I the pilot only slugged a handful of shots at the shindig, and our pre-party drinking was uncharacteristically subdued. The conditions seemed right for the skittish Gerry. Plus in his favor: the journey was only a mile; what could go wrong in a mile? His hesitation was all of five seconds, but at that moment the 1200 bits of pre-college advice his mother drummed into his head had instantly registered, and it showed in his twitching face. He smiled, joked, then playfully relented, yelling, "Move over assholes!" He scrambled over the bodies piled next to each other, then stiffly reclined by the far wall.

The thing is, his stress level was teeming, and it was difficult to conceal. I could smell it drifting forward in the van, all the pherperonens or whatever the fuck they're called accumulating and sending a charge in me—by God at that moment I was finally fully ready to party. I who for the life of me could not get myself up for that pity-filled gathering we just attended became belatedly kicked-in and ready to go. The engine was cranked and revved to 9000 rpms, and the rearview mirror rotated downwards so I could watch old Gerry on the trip. He seemed to sense a reciprocation of adrenaline, and sagged a bit. The mirror had to even be clicked down another notch. He was lying on the floor of the van treading hopelessly in a sea of beer cans. He was fragily perched on bony elbows in windowless agony, unable to shout warnings of the oncoming truck, unable to even watch any advancement of his demise. It would now come as suddenly as a friendly wink, leaving his youthful, undeserving body cold and in a heap, until the forces of nature disintegrated it altogether. He peered longingly at the side door now walled shut with bodies, then surreptitiously scanned the opposite wall for some type of emergency exit. To leave now would be to lose face; to stay could be to lose his entire *head*. There really was no choice but to lie back and pray.

I of course felt obligated to give Gerry the ride of his life. I cupped my hands around my mouth and exhaled, then instantaneously snorted the carbon dioxide with my nostrils. By my calculations I was give-or-take a .07 or .08 BAC level, near ideal driving conditions. Wilt was strapped to the captain's chair on my right; he would help with the foggy navigation. The van was groggy out of the gate—loaded with 1200 pounds of cargo the six-cylinder engine accelerated like an old lady in a caddie, which appeared to reassure Gerry. Perhaps it wasn't as he remembered at all, maybe too many or too few beers or the remnants of test anxiety caused the fear and trepidation of his last excursion. Or maybe his driver had finally outgrown such juvenile and potentially hazardous tendencies.

Quashing such notions, the van after a half-minute leveled out at 80, which seemed a comfortable cruising speed down the narrow College Avenue. The other cars introduced a slalom course. The vehicle downshifted into second at 60 locking the wheels briefly on the wet pavement with a beg of the engine for mercy, then after a tap of the breaks arced a 40 mph right angle into a narrow alley near Safeway—shortcut—with the truck trampolining up the sidewalk gradient and the tires leveling scattered beer cans with quick pops.

Nothing produces a more noticeable collective gasp from the floor passengers than the heralded trampoline effect. With Gerry though it was oddly a high-pitched "Hey!" sounding like a friendly greeting. Wilt wheeled and waved back. A shopping cart nosed its way into the tight street from an alley; proving an uncanny knowledge of the vehicle's width we decided to blitzkrieg past it at one cunt hair—that didn't happen—the wayward cart somehow grazed the corner of the hood and slammed into a dumpster. It was the cart's fault, we concluded, and we thankfully had seven witnesses minus Gerry to back the story up.

We reached the Westfall Hall parking lot in record time. The brainpower that comes into play at this point is deciding which driveway to take to enter the lot; I opted for the second one. No what-the-hell the first one and the van again at 40 lurched leftwards for the entrance and we would have made it cleanly except for the goddamned vinyl seat—the slick, smooth, Armor-alled poorly constructed American seat which when coupled with Gap denim jeans offers no traction whatsoever. And due to this engineering flaw I the pilot became mercilessly hurled on the floor next to the engine cover, trying to steer the thing from the vantage point of old Gerry himself. The van hit the curb and impressively rode diagonally on two wheels for a full second. The interesting thing is that Gerry's nearly new Camaro, parked worlds away from the other vehicles to avoid door dings, came within three feet of meeting its maker from an old van loaded with 1200 additional pounds of battering power. Or so I was told—I was steering from the floor remember.

17

Van was okay, for all those concerned. I needed a new rim, that's about it. My van watches over my friends and me. It's truly one of the most amazing cars I've met. And the perfect college vehicle. I had attended Whittier College in California right out of high school but was carless and immature, receiving shitty grades and getting stoned all the time, so I took a year off and worked to save for a van. I actually wanted a van and a motocross bike, with dreams of racing professionally, but ended up affording just the old van, making do with my outdated bike. It's a white, very dependable 1977 Dodge with windows all around—seemingly your standard old painter's van. Or at least that's what it wants people to believe. For inside, van has a heart of a lion.

We have a rare car/driver relationship. Van looks out for me like a big brother. Be it a cross-country trip or just a shaky late-night jaunt across town, it's never let me down. On one ski trip to Vail, van cruised 500 miles without incident; exactly one block from the dorm a tire started to flatten. She limped the rest of the way home so I could change it.

Perks abound. A perfect bottle opener is disguised as a door hinge. The floor ingeniously slopes slightly towards all six doors, employing an automatic self-cleaning mechanism. It allows a few of the hundreds of beer cans scattered about to fall out each time a door is opened, ensuring the cans don't pile so high as to constitute a safety hazard. Van's body is made of tough, bulletproof metal. So when you accidentally run into shopping carts, the evidence is barely noticeable in the morning.

Van's best attribute is its Clark Kent demeanor. Cops just don't want to bother with hassling Mr. Nice Guy on the road. It always looks like it's innocuously chugging home from a Local 346 meeting. The pot smoke could be thick as gravy inside, but the truck's cheery headlights and friendly grill never betray what's going on.

It's a three-on-the-tree with a loud, whiny engine. Second gear has all kinds of engine braking when you're off the gas. The 225 six-cylinder engine has no acceleration whatsoever; it compensates by screaming comically so you think it's working its ball joints off. But once the speed is up, van handles curves like a slightly pregnant sports car, never wallowing unpredictably. Van also has a bed and curtains all around, including the front, for added privacy the dorms often can't offer.

Its reserve tank is monstrous. In college, the gas gauge has yet to read over "E." The sucker will read "E" for months; I'll finally scrape together a couple bucks to feed it and it'll still say "E," but it's a minute variation of "E." That's so I know it's not broken. Uninitiated sorts would borrow the car and fret it was out of gas, unaware of the intricate gradation scale incorporated in the fuel gauge. I'd assure them not to worry, whereas van, feeling no need to exert itself for a stranger, would promptly sputter and die three blocks away.

Tyce has a Ford Granada he nicknamed "The Gray Ghost." A third of the rationale behind the name is the car's color; the remainder is an enigma. The Ford too has a gas gauge that never sees the light of day. But its design is a joke. Here's the difference: The needle on my vehicle never descends below the letter "E" regardless of the tank's emptiness, usually diagonally cutting the "E" right down the middle. Once the needle actually erases the vertical line of the letter, your next trip has gotta be for the gas station. It's an uncomplicated, logical design.

Conversely, Tyce's gas gauge is nearly useless. When *his* car is moderately empty, which is always, the needle plummets *below* the "E," with the stupid thing actually leaning against the bar on the left. It's impossible to discern the true emptiness of the piece of shit. It might have an entire gallon left; it might be on fumes. It's like a worst-case scenario needle, and makes driving the car unsettling. One thing is clear: the car obviously was targeted for people before they entered or after they graduated college.

The Gray Ghost was seldom free from adventure with Tyce behind the wheel, especially when his brain was bobbing about in various degrees of stonedness. One (typical) Saturday night Tyce was smoking an abnormally large amount of pot at a friend's. He and his buddy were bonging like the liberty bell. Many students choose to forgo pot on a weekend party night since it can enhance introversion later at a party, but Tyce stood apart from this crowd. Tyce could attend class and give verbal presentations while high. He could pick up women while high. He could study effectively while high. In short, he was a very capable individual while stoned. It was damn near enviable. On this occasion, however, he was taking pot smoking to an entirely different level.

Tyce somehow happened on a bud that was enormous. It was the size of a California artichoke. It would have lasted the average Joe a full fall semester, with a pipe load left for New Years. The thing was so moist and sticky, it took some muscle to detach a piece. He and his friend Mildew were determinedly trying to pare it down this evening, so it was at least transportable. Around 10:00 p.m., a buddy Paul and three others stopped by Mildew's place with an offer. "There's a party across town—it's supposed to be a rager. You guys interested?" It was the two's first post-bonging encounter with the real world. Tyce gazed at Paul cross-eyedly. It took a good while just converting the sounds from Paul's mouth into usable information. It was like cracking a foreign code.

When everything finally gelled, Tyce leapt on the idea, bravely ignoring his debilitated condition.

"Let's roll!" Paul thought the time lapse was just mulling over whether or not to go. It was a foolish assumption—Tyce would knowingly blow off a party for only one reason: if he was tied up at some *other* bash. And even then it wouldn't occur without some guilt.

So he and Mildew drifted to the parking lot, fired up The Gray Ghost, and prepared to follow the four in the other car. Tyce tooted the generic Ford horn. "Hold on, I need gas," he yelled across the lot. The moment reassured the two riders in the Ghost, for it provided evidence that at least one decision-making zone of Tyce's brain was still functioning. Tyce hyperventilated, then, with extreme focus, glided the vehicle across the street to the station and alongside the pump. Thankfully, he still remembered how to drive. He carefully exited the car and walked towards the mini mart to buy the fuel. His 20 years of life-practice in walking and taking wallets out of pockets ensured that his sub-conscious would handle these basics. He removed a crisp one-dollar bill from his wallet, and successfully handed it to the clerk. The act, he figured, was like one correctly placed building block. When each successive building block of the journey was stacked evenly to the top, they'd be at the party. It was as simple as that. He fired up the Ghost; the gas needle slept soundly, making no acknowledgement. And the two cars zoomed off for the party.

It took forever to get there. Ten, 20, 30 minutes passed on the road. Tyce's eyes were slits. It took using some extra facial muscles to keep the lids open enough just to see. His mind wanted to hallucinate, to confuse the objects on the road with objects that didn't exist. He lectured himself internally with affirmations, attempting a methodic antidote to the clouded state he'd labored all day to achieve. His hands exerted hundreds of foot-pounds of pressure on the steering wheel. They were soggy with sweat, resembling bathtub hands. He bent over nearly flush to the windshield, practically steaming the thing up. It allowed a closer, more-intense view of the situation. His concentration had to be 100 percent. Mildew turned up the radio—Tyce vetoed the move, shutting it down. Focus was the thing here, to get this spacecraft safely landed at the party. His saving grace was the fact that no navigational efforts were required—luckily his job was simply to follow Paul's taillights wherever they went, and bingo!—he'd reach his destination.

Tyce was starting to get pissed. Had he known the party was this far out he would have put more gas in the Ghost. Or maybe blown the whole thing off. They were in the boonies. They passed up Horsetooth Reservoir, passed the football stadium in front of the foothills. He bore down on the red taillights, winding through back roads, turning left, right, even U-turning a few times. Huge meadows graced the side of the moonlit road, packed with sleeping cows. This better be a damn good bash, he thought. They were so far from town, that maybe five minutes elapsed with no traces of human life other than the two-car caravan.

They reached a four-way stop. His buddy's car stayed put. Tyce waited patiently behind them. "I knew it—the bastards are lost." He gave them a minute to check maps and the like. After a long while, Paul got out of his car and headed towards Tyce's to break the already evident news. Paul was wielding a large bat or stick of some sort. It looked menacingly out of place. Tyce's mind raced. The blonde with the dimples last night—could that have been *Paul's* chick, he wondered? Paranoia kicked in. It was all an elaborate plan to ensure Tyce would never screw *anyone* again, *ever*.

"What the hell are you following me for, asshole?" It wasn't Paul at all. Tyce quickly discovered that a) he was tailing a person he'd never seen before and b) it was impossible to articulate exactly why he was following the guy on every back street in northern Colorado.

Large amounts of pot can play games with the sensible mind. It's like this: The mind in general has two lists of things to think about. One list covers the essentials you need for basic survival in life—studying for a test, doing a job properly, ordering a pizza, etc. Practical, problem-solving stuff. The other list addresses the "non-essentials"— creative mulling that adds color to life and creates separation, distinction from most other animals. Pot does wonders for the latter list. Back-road journeys to vacation spots of the thought processes are commonplace. Revelations occur, and meaningful chunks of life are "figured out" while under the influence. Unfortunately, its effects aren't as reliable with the former list. In fact, the drug can take the rational mind and scramble it up, like an egg. Things like remembering the first part of your sentence can take extraordinary effort.

Tyce could have been colorful with this gentleman, whoever the hell he was. Logic was another story. It was a fine line: He could have discussed why we are here, as a species; he just couldn't explain why he was there, following the stranger up and down the countryside. He was caught off guard, and the words wouldn't quite form. He rehearsed the syllables in his mind, but they didn't seem exactly right. Too many vowels, too few consonants. He just stared forth mutely, at the way the guy's eyebrows arced across his face.

Tyce turned towards the view out of the windshield and rolled the window to the top, ridding himself of the unpleasantness to his left. He slowly backed the car up, and wheeled it around. He saw the man with the baseball bat in his rear view mirror, getting smaller. The guy was much less intimidating at this height. But having solved that predicament, three challenges still loomed before him: 1) He'd have to make it back to campus without the benefit of the red taillights. 2) He'd easily burnt the dollar in gas, and there sure weren't any gas stations in these parts. 3) He hadn't a clue where the fuck he was.

Tyce somehow stumbled on a convenience store, like a desert traveler onto an oasis. His mouth luckily was somewhat functional now, and was able to request directions. "The college. Which way?!" was enough to get him pointed in the correct direction. Next, he began fixating on the thought of Westfall Hall—one of the two "towers" on campus. It was the tallest building in the region and was lit up like a Christmas tree—it could be seen for miles. Thoughts of the towers now assumed the former role of the taillights, easing Tyce's mind. Their presence, somewhere on a horizon, provided the hope and security required to complete the journey home. They were like a newfound mother's teat. Once they appeared, everything would be back to normal. And they did, and, of course, it was.

18

Tyce and all the AOPers had the witlessness to regularly mire ourselves in situations like these, yet enough luck to ensure no serious consequences ever resulted from them. I'm not sure if it's luck or what. That's the simple explanation, a writing-off of more complicated forces at work. It just seems that when we've done one stupid thing too many, when we've stepped way over the line of stupidity into the land of nothing but the stupid, something saves us. Some days it seems AOP comes stock with a built-in force field. I'll be lazy and just call it luck Tyce has known he's lucky from day one; in fact he's revolved much of his college experience around this realization.

Exactly one week after the Great Bud incident, a tremendous ice storm hit Fort Collins. The treachery of the driving didn't deter Tyce and Don from downing plenty of beer and hopping in The Gray Ghost to see what was up at a friend's. The road was slicker than an Olympic skating rink. To make the journey even more formidable, a joint made the rounds. The resulting dry mouth from the joint was accurately relieved with more beer, with the empties piled high in the back. Tyce was a fairly cautious driver to begin with, but in these conditions he was barely chugging. This tiptoeing around like a ballerina became tedious for Don. "You drive like my mother," he challenged. Tyce knew the mark of an insult, even when mired in a compromised state of mind. He punched the pedal and the back end of the Ghost obediently spun around, slamming into the bumper of a Cadillac in the next lane.

The Caddie's driver was a woman of taste and character who worked in the front office of the Denver Broncos. Tyce promptly identified himself as "Joe Peterson," apologizing that his license, insurance card, registration and other incriminating papers were in absentia. The woman of class didn't like the circumstance, thinking it fishy, and chose to involve the cops on her car phone. This made the boys sweat since they were just the fair side of wasted, had beer cans lining the car's interior and were suspending helplessly from a bald-faced lie. The onset of the situation required poise and composure, Tyce instead delivered imprudence and folly. He again found it impossible to differentiate between the cartoon world he inhabited and a real situation of dire consequence. The cops would now come and take his toys away. The minutes the elegant woman was on the phone were tension-filled for the lads, especially devoid of brewskies. Even Don had a concerned look for the first time ever. The woman hung up the receiver and walked sullenly towards the two dunderheads. She reported that the police could only respond to emergency calls, given the weather. She could do nothing but scribble down Mr. Peterson's name, address and the license plate number, and take off.

Tyce, with the resolve to cross the "t"s and dot the "i"s in the caper, shaved his mustache clean the minute he got home. How could she ever identify him now? His lunacy snowballed. He took the thing as far as it could go. "What in God's name happened to your car?" his father demanded to know the following weekend. Tyce went with the sure thing: "It was lent in good faith to Joe Peterson who dented it." Any mortal fool would have at worst got thrown in jail over the incident, and at best suffered inflated insurance rates and enormous fines.

Inexplicably however, the polished woman never traced the car's plates, never even followed up on the situation. This seemed not to surprise Tyce much, and his world continued its oblong spin, refreshingly free from requisite moral lesson.

We realized later on that Joe Peterson has always hung out with the AOPers. The broken fire-extinguisher glass? The bastard Peterson. The vomit in the stairwell? Ol' weak-stomached Joe. He became a menace to right-minded folk everywhere.

19

Picking up a girl is the crown achievement for the male college student, and is the centerpiece and logical culmination of the Art of Partying. If such a challenge were removed from AOP, the entire thing would become stale and ultimately pointless. A night of partying without bringing a member of the opposite sex home is considered, by AOP's tough standard, a failed night. It may have been a raucous, outrageous, drink-slamming affair, but it's technically a bust none-the-less.

For the college student, finding a woman to take home is an aggregate study of aesthetics, sociology, psychology and look-ma-no-hands ejaculation, in that order. And a more engaging study session can't be had. For, barring any major food addictions, the college-aged female form is invariably beautiful. It's nature's finest work. The more women seen in the half-light of the dawn, clad in sexily smeared makeup and partially draped sheet, the more apparent it becomes. Every breast has its own shape and texture, each navel a novel swirl and depth. They're the perfect complement to the extra-horny, just wakened, clouded, 6 a.m. need-to-take-a-piss state of semi-sobriety. And in the soft, dusty light beam, with your friend sweetly sleeping on her stomach, three hours of sleep suffice, and two fingers begin a wispy journey across her body. They glide down the river of slightly tangled hair that splashes on her back, then slip down the little ski slope from the shoulder blades towards the short little crack of the ass. As she eyes-closedly rolls over, tugging the cover high in mock modesty, as the sheet jiggles in one breasty bounce, is the silhouetted form before you not the grandest, most erotic sight on earth? And during all this, she's still pretending she's asleep.

The art of picking up a woman at a party or bar is a complex one. The challenge of course is to take her home that night. Most anyone can get laid spending all his beer money on several dates with a chick. This is wasteful behavior and conflicts with AOP philosophy. It's also boringly routine. For an intimate encounter with a never-before-met partner of the opposite sex is a uniquely rewarding experience for both parties. But until the sociological undercurrents of male/female behavior is studied, the process is also is a highly difficult one.

Our species in short has biological needs and societal needs. Biologically, we're programmed to perpetuate the species, and then die. The male attempts to spread his seed whenever and wherever possible, and the female selectively responds to whomever she deems is the fittest candidate. The male is continually horny; the female's horniness often falls victim to her intense fluctuations of hormonal activity. Even a repressed chick with "no sex drive" wants to screw when she ovulates—it's the moment when Mother Nature takes her aside and whispers, "Quit being such an old maid—spread 'em!" In general, however, the humping fever can run as strong for women as for men, but cultural limits are imposed. Society's customs unfairly don't allow the fairer gender to directly express or respond to this natural drive. Ladies want sex, but a stigma of being used when love isn't attached to the act is present. This, of course, is mostly a societal creation, but since most of us adhere to some social construct, it's difficult to disregard.

Finding a woman for the night is a very different process than the search for a long- term mate. Most failed attempts at one-night-stands mistakenly employ long-term search techniques. They re-weave the web of standard social tradition, thus are inherently destined for failure. For example, plying the woman with attention and buying her drinks and roses from the flower lady might result in a future date if she fancies such crap, but solves nothing for the evening at hand. The more she's thrust in the traditional role, the more bonded she becomes to the very conventions you're supposed to be disarming. Immersing her in social custom dictates she act in a prescribed way—i.e. trading phone numbers and splitting for the night with her girlfriend.

Key theories AOPers use are the Strength Through Indifference (STI) model and the Displacement of Power (DOP) theorem. In the STI model, only modest interest is ever conveyed to a just-met woman, regardless of the degree she makes your heart pound. You're vaguely consumed yes, infatuated, no. All signs or intimations that you're smitten are deathblows. In this 3/4-attentioned zone, uniqueness is key. Every point in the conversation should veer in an unanticipated direction. Any chick overwhelmed by it all isn't going home with you anyway. Women too often are chronically bored with their worlds; it's your mission to assemble a new one for them and give them a brief, unpretentious tour. For garish attempts to impress are detected by the most naive women, and are rejected by the most dog faced. A strutting, egotistical demeanor and appearance guarantee early good-byes. A cliched compliment fails here, an unusual one strikes pay dirt (you've got great eyebrows). Unconventionality generally pays off—the further she's detached her from the everyday world, the quicker she'll release it from her grasps.

All that Dale Carnagie crap works fine for securing long-term relationships; it works in reverse here. For example, while Carnagie might promote unwavering eye contact, AOP is partial to periodic surveyings of the field during conversation. Too *much* eye contact conjures images of a smooth talking, far-too-interested dick salesman. And nothing's wrong with stutters and impromptu ponderings; a slightly flawed, sincere human struggling in rumination is lots more palatable than an over enthusiastic, extra-confident clown with rehearsed lines.

Take huge chances. I have, and haven't gotten slapped yet. If you've been playing eye-contact games with a chick all night, walk up to her (when she's alone) and sweetly and innocently plant a kiss on her cheek. Kissing a woman before speaking with her is a magical thing. And it illustrates the singleness of the club atmosphere—it's a glorious experiment in nonverbal communication. The loud music requires it. The way one dances, the way one walks, the manner in which one clings to a peer group like a life-support system—entire personalities are disclosed with no words uttered. It's the domain of AOP, replete with twisted rules and illogical outcomes. Some garrulous sort can sweat through half a night working a chick with practiced charm and jokes, only to lose her to some bastard who walks up and makes out with her without one prior word or many after. It's a terrifically undemocratic situation.

Two essential points:

1) It sounds cruel (and cheap), but it bears repeating: *never* buy your friend a drink, at least initially. Once she's locked in it's okay to do so, but if it's done right off the bat, you're finished. It puts her in the power seat initially, making you the desperate stranger begging for a ride. Let all the other idiots loosen up the ladies with alcohol, and watch as they thank them for the drink and guiltlessly head for the opposite corner of the bar.

2) If you ask a woman to dance before eye contact has been established, she'll most likely be caught in automatic reject mode, which good-looking women in a club quickly fall into. It's a state created by

getting hit-on to dance hundreds of times an hour. They'll eventually say no before the thought even goes through processing.

Many forms of eye contact exist; these are some:

- *The Reinforce-the-Ego Look*: The goal here is to verify that one is still attractive to the opposite sex. It's a message received rather than transmitted, and it's important to not confuse the difference. REL begins by two people walking towards each other from a good distance, where initial eye contact is established. The REL person then diverts the gaze downward, until she senses that you, her guinea pig, are around 20 feet away. She then reinstates the eye contact, but only to see if she's being checked out. Then, to indicate she's got better plans than to waste time with you, she looks off and motors ahead.

- *The One-Second Look*: The one-second eye contact across the room is rather standard in a club or party, and doesn't necessarily denote interest without a follow up. However, a third and fourth one-seconder firmly implies, "So ya gonna ask me to dance or what?" If the girl behind the third and fourth one-seconder declines a dance, feel privileged to press the issue.

- *The Mismatched-Dancing-Partner Look:* Be careful of this siren. She's the one who while grinding a slow dance is making deep eyes with a dude grinding his slow dance. High potential for getting in a scrap with somebody.

- *The Chick-Who-Looks-Then-Says-Something-to-Her-Friend-Who-Looks Look*: A good opportunity with either looker. Lots of women's interests are reinforced by the opinion of their friend/group. It's a fact that a woman often will show zero interest in someone until it's discovered her friends are smitten. Just like that, she's likewise in love.

- *The Who-Can-Hold-it-the-Longest Look:* Occasionally you'll hook stares with someone who won't release. Anything over five seconds gets gnarly—it's as close to physical contact as there is without actually touching. She's either yours for the taking or someone actually in as dire need of attention from the opposite sex as you yourself.

Once eye contact and the ensuing introductions are made, The Displacement of Power (DOP) theorem kicks in. DOP seeks to put the chick in the driver's seat, increasing her comfort level. DOP's boon is that it works for all personality types, even socially insecure ones. Shyness is the great bane of those afflicted, yet when used properly it can actually enhance pick-up situations; it's because of DOP. Such a trait makes one appear non-threatening, and invokes a maternal instinct from your friend. Direct or aggressive behavior automatically raises a woman's guard in club situations, pushing her back; reticent, enigmatic behavior elicits interest, begging her to reach within. The idea here is to create a role-reversal where suddenly *she's* the interested one, and you're wondering whether to hang or move on. Known as the WHOOSH effect in AOP-speak, veterans can pinpoint the moment this shift occurs—it's a near-tangible feeling. She's cruising along in control and feeling secure, which is the precise moment an innocent offer is made to check out a great song at your place, one you're certain she'd love. She's there, always.

The inability to culminate the scene at this point takes a small mountain of bad chemistry. Such a dramatic turnabout should be rare. One way to ensure she spends the night is picking up an eight-pound jug of cheap wine on the way home, then swilling it down together. Who is she to ask a drunk to drive her home? But it should now be realized she's not averse to sleeping with you, even if the notion is still ensnared in the recesses of her mind. The key thing here is to be an awesome kisser. Women staunchly opposed to one-night-stands make amazing turnabouts when biology kicks in and their crotches dampen. And nothing assists that effect better than proper make-out technique.

The kiss is beyond a prelude to love making. It's the main ingredient, before and during. If lovemaking were candy, the kiss would be the sugar. The perfect kiss is such a grand, erotic experience, it's a tragedy some folks are so inept at its technique. One of the great conundrums in life is this: Can a bad kisser somehow transform into a good kisser, or are they forever doomed? Sometimes people get this mixed-up with head. Many women do not begin with the ability to give flawless head, but develop the skill quite estimably through research and practice. But bad kissing is a whole 'nother subject.

Who knows even where to begin with educating the lousy kisser? Kissing is the most personal of acts—far more personal than any head job (which is the reason a hooker will do the latter rather than the former). So all intimations of improvement are inherently insulting, creating a delicate, maddening situation. It's true, the contorted face and squirming body language of the recipient convey that *something's* wrong. But only the problem rather than the remedy gets addressed.

Dwelling on it, it's bizarre that bad kissers haven't a fucking clue of their inabilities. They somehow believe the zero satisfaction, the complete absence of pleasure delivered and received after committing a full attack with mouth fully agape and tongue wagging violently is what kissing's all about. They're a curious breed. So the riddle lurks: If certain folks are unable to generate their own enjoyments from the most natural of experiences, is it possible to artificially create these pleasures for these sorts through tutorage?

Let's review the methods of the good kiss and the horrible kiss, and examine various preventions of the latter. It should be noted initially that certain physical attributes are of course required for any decent smooch. The kisser with a scant top and/or bottom lip can never fulfill expectation, regardless of technique. These lip types sadly have only a practical function, which is sealing off the mouth from dust and other shit outside the body.

Like sex, the great kiss *gradually* builds to its raging climax. The experience begins feather-lightly, in almost a controlled tease. As her soft, sweet, half-dry/half-moist lips slowly mesh with yours, composure and restraint begin to erode, and mutual invitations inside are presented. The tongues gently brush against each other, and the salty taste introduces yet another erotic sensation. Its acceleration is cued by momentary stimulation. Other erogenous zones like the neck and ears are sought, in solo trade-offs. Dominant and submissive roles are swapped—all integral aspects in kissing, foreplay and sex.

The shitty kiss, in stark contrast, offers no foundation on which to build. Nearly all begin the same way: in high gear with the mouth jacked fully open, converting two comely lips into one giant pink sphere. As the sphere advances towards you, two choices emerge. The first is to attempt making out with one of her lips, an experience that's 1) somewhat unsatisfying and 2) fucking ridiculous. The second choice is to crank open your own mouth to a similar diameter, in an all-out search for the wayward lips somewhere north and south of the intended area. Unfortunately, lips stretched to this position invariably transform into two flattened bands of immaleable muscle. And when the four rigid components finally do hook up, the nonexistent sensuousness is extraordinary.

The next step in this nightmare involves a desperate effort to reel her lips in, to find something salvageable in the mayhem. With methodical guidance, the offending jaw can usually be retracted to a reasonable distance, but it generally springs ajar again within seconds, like a busted bear trap. Here it becomes apparent the kisser has not experienced the rewards of the proper kiss, and may never be able to. The irony is that the transgressor's intentions are rife with fervor; sadly, this is the *only* sensation conveyed. And to finally address the question concerning reform? Hell if I know—I've never had the bravery or commitment to express discontent, at least verbally.

Incidentally, if one suspects she/he may have mega-mouth tendencies, the golf ball test works best. At some point during the first five seconds of making out, freeze your face. Slowly extract it from your partner's, and pick up a golf ball. If you can insert it cleanly in your mouth, you're fucking up royally.

It's possible that lousy kissers might be victims of too much movie watching. Film is expensive, and too often the characters skip the essential early and mid stages of the kiss. Such a kiss can look stimulating on screen, but fails miserably in real life. Once again, it's an area where head and the kiss are often confused. Porn films are a capital way for a young woman to learn proper head technique; with the kiss, basic instinct should be the guide.

These are the other variations of the crappy smooch:

The Tight-Lipped Smoocher: This is simply the full-mouth extension in reverse. These are divided souls who offer the kiss while simultaneously shutting down any further activity. It's a psychological phenomenon worthy of research. It's like the chick who invites you in her bedroom so she can push you the hell out the window into the flowerbed.

The Chewer: Gentle lip gnawing can accentuate any kiss. But these people act like they've missed lunch.

The Tongue Thruster: Tongue work is the fine art of kissing. But when hyper- extended, the visiting tongue takes on a rigid, missile-like quality that causes the host tongue to recoil in fright to an area near the tonsils. This inspires the visiting tongue to probe about even more violently, causing a near war in the goddamned mouth.

To avoid all such scenarios, making out with your friend early on is essential. The result provides a blueprint for the remainder of the night. It's a tragedy, but a person who can't kiss is nearly always an inept lover. And, like an unfortunate born with an incurable affliction, there's probably little that can remedy it.

20

It's understandable that a woman may angrily deduce that this pick-up section might be for some misogynist to get his rocks off through bullshit and deception. That crap is as far from AOP as you can get. Besides the odious moral implications, such a style, simply, is scripted for failure anyway. First off, women are far more intuitive then men, and can usually spot frauds (and misogynists) miles away. Everyone's heard stories of great Casanova bullshitters who regularly declare their everlasting love to women only to score. Chances are that these people are bullshitting you as well. Such behavior triggers the date game, begging the girl to *resist* sex on the first night, fucking your lights out only after you've sprung for a lobster dinner. Conversely, it's necessary for an AOPer to state an *aversion* to commitment during the course of the night. Two or three times, minimally. It solves any issues of potential regret on her side of the bed, and paves the way for an enduring physical friendship.

So, for the fellows regularly left solo piloting on a late Saturday night, try sincerity and honesty about your intentions for a change. You'll be pleasantly surprised. Lots of women on campus appreciate a non-committal, hedonistic lifestyle as much as their male counterparts. They just don't want to feel used or lied to in the process.

Disclaimers aside, if you think you're doing everything right in this game and are still failing miserably, it's quite possible you're simply too ugly. Smoke a joint to obtain a degree of objectivity, then plant your face a foot from the mirror for a few minutes. Is it all squashed together like the top part of a pumpkin? Start twitching your mustache area—are you beginning to look like a rodent? If you play connect-the-dots with your zits, is the resulting line over a meter? Tie a string taught from earlobe to earlobe—does it cut straight across the face or at some steep angle? Do your eyebrows connect? (I'm talking about the *long* way around).

Sometimes non-ugly ordinary Joes have the toughest time of all. Good looking enough to believe they'll strike pay dirt, plain faced enough to hear the last call at the bar every goddamned night. Try this test: assemble a big, closed-mouth grin on your mug. Be truthful: any resemblance to the "Have a Nice Day" smiley face? After these analyses, it may be necessary to seek a long-term girlfriend or to join a frat and let the organization pick someone out for you. Yet I've seen homely guys pick up their share of girls, though their methods require a much more aggressive system than the one espoused here. They play a high numbers game, like a salesman that closes one out of 200 calls. These are thick-skinned sorts and should be commended on their amazing immunity to humiliation and rejection.

If looks *don't* appear to be linked to your pick-up woes, choice of venue and time management are usually the issues at hand.

- Choice of Venue

It's worth protesting, but the best clubs with the coolest music are the places where one is least likely to pick up a woman. Smokey, stylish blues bars are it for the tunes, but simply don't cater to the singles scene. The places with the most irritating, thumping songs conceivable are where the beautiful girls can be found. These joints feature tunes as vehicles for dancing; it's a quantum jump from real music. The sounds are featured so no distraction from the matter at hand occurs, which is meeting that special someone to spend the night with. There's no chance that musical preoccupations will mess with your strategies and tactics. The brain can actually accept the sonic assault because of the hodgepodge of other stimuli at hand—namely comely, sparsely dressed women. Were these stimuli removed, the environment would be torturous.

Though the place defies our character, recently a few AOPers discovered that the classy bar works surprisingly well as a pick-up venue. It may be necessary to dust off the prom suit for this one, but the payoff can be worth it. The aforementioned dance clubs have the inherent disadvantage of being advertised meat markets, with each woman poised to repel hundreds of attempted hits from every loser in the joint. A general defensiveness is employed, which often isn't easily shed when someone worthwhile comes along. Women in the classy bar don't need to construct such safeguards, and can be more prone to making eye contact, initiating conversation and taking off with you. The big disadvantage here is the phony suit-clad competition bumping about the place.

- Time Management

One of the toughest things to discern, especially in an acutely buzzed state, is whether to pursue the chick you've met at 10:30 p.m. or to gamble for a hotter one and risk whacking off at 3:00 a.m. It's especially difficult when the party or club is a good one. It's easy to assume that if she's really smitten, you can check out other avenues and return if need be. And if mutual interest is demonstrated only through eye contact; short, superficial dialogue; and/or a quick dance, then she *is* fair game for the entire night. Unfortunately, if you connect through personal conversation for over five minutes, an odd degree of responsibility or commitment is inherited, and if you leave and expect to return down the line, she'll act like an ex-wife stiffed on child-support checks.

Two factors determine directions here, following two too-elementary principles: personality and looks. Personality-wise, it's mainly important that the chick hasn't immersed herself in a molded social situation from which she can't or won't escape, like a sorority. Like great patriots, these girls' allegiances are generally so group-oriented, that even apart from their gaggle they'll exhort simple, group-minded observations and behaviors. They're sadly like a script free from improvisation. Luckily, these types are usually recognizable by their pack, so it's rare your and their time can be wasted.

Along with the requirement that the woman possesses an original, curious personality is an informal physical-assessment system AOP uses: the One-Great-Feature standard. Does she have a perfect ass? Or are her tits well shaped and firm? Or is she the perfect kisser? Or maybe her eyes are deadly? While one-night-stands aren't requiring of the full package, OGF guidelines are generally met.

If the 10:30 p.m. woman is cool, OGF, and with a friend your buddy's interested in, AOP believes in securing the sure thing. While AOP often favors the gambler, only a foolish long shotter would abandon this situation. It's actually the perfect Friday night scenario. If you decide to commit, there's plenty of time to determine the chick's intentions to avoid getting burnt later on. Lacing the conversation with playful sexual innuendo at this point reveals the level of her prudishness. If she cracks any dick-sucking jokes, you've essentially struck gold. It's now okay to round up some drinks for her, but with care. A woman puking out the window on the ride home creates an inverse proportion, increasing your chance of getting pulled over by the cops and reducing by equal amounts any chances of intimacy. If drinks are needed and money's short, you'll have to borrow a pitcher of beer on a table temporarily deserted by dancers. Reaching for three-quarter full individual drinks is strictly a last resort. Try and do this while your friend is taking a leak or at least looking the other way, you cheap bastard.

If perchance midnight strikes, however, and no prospects are in sight, it's time to jump into full gear. It's essential not to panic at this juncture. Realize the women are drunker, looser and more hardcore than the ones now home and asleep. By now, at least some casual contacts should have been established, and the tone of the place determined and tweaked, if possible. This is important. All gatherings like these take on a singular life of their own, a sort of group mind, and veteran AOPers must be adept at their interpretation.

People generally require mass approval before allowing themselves to shift out of their customary driving gear. If they witness lots of sordid activity taking place, their own moral standard degenerates, at least for the duration of the party. Mardi Gras is a prime example of this type of mass "deviance." Stick the most upstanding, lock-legged puritanical girl amid the festivities, give her a few drinks, and in an hour she'll be flashing her tits to anyone caring to see them, like the rest of the gang. The girls without a bevy of earned Mardi Gras beads around their necks are the standouts here, ignominiously perceived as joyless, undesired prudes by everybody else. For a short time, moral turpitude assumes the norm. It's an amazing sociological phenomenon, yet, upon reflection, rather understandable.

For with all our country's ravings of the importance of individual freedoms, we're strangely a repressed, hung-up lot. We've got plenty of freedom, just not the balls to use it. In fact, anyone acting *too* free is considered some sort of flake. The large number of political freedoms we possess are offset by the even greater amount of outdated moral laws still on the books. It's this vigorous social policing by a formidable gang of old maids blanketing the north continent that never allows anything to get too out of hand.

Yet when people are given the chance to express themselves freely in a microcosmically accepting social structure, many will do so with abandon. They'll behave like malnourished souls finally discovering an elixir. So, on a miniature scale, lessons of Mardi Gras are valuable to any AOPer. It's the perfect model of the chasm between the things we are and the things we need. And proof of how easily the masses, with the right stimuli, can be influenced and redirected on certain levels.

In college this syndrome can be extended to The Party, which too can sway individual outcomes. Wilt always makes a hearty effort at the breakdown of this universal mind. He'll make geometrically spiraled rounds, presenting literally every woman in the joint with a temporary offbeat slice of life. His bizarre manner often borders on intrusion, a crash of a nonexistent party, so defenses can automatically arise. Yet armed with the conviction of a demented Jehovah's Witness spreading the gospel of kicks and enlightenment, he happily weathers any rejections. And over the course of the night these women, witnessing the man's unbridled energies focused on the opposite sex, eventually exert their naturally competitive instincts and vie madly for his attention. Entering the world of the same guy considered wacky on arrival. Wilt, in search of his own kicks, unwittingly changes such people momentarily, allowing them to bask in some mental recess they clearly rejected hours earlier.

Most women at a party or bar into the wee hours have some degree of free-spiritedness anyway. But everyone is fair game. In fact, a strange equilibrium exists in the most prudish women. The more severe their repression, the more devout they are in their studies, the more helpless they happen to be against ongoing fantasies of getting gang-banged by the debating team. And their chaste, church-going life style offers no defense when such reveries come knocking without invitation. It goes with the territory—the more forbidden something is, the more enticing and erotic it often becomes. So these people are like walking sex machines. Imagine: no masturbation. No copulation. Multiply it all by 21 years, and you've got a time bomb waiting to explode.

Here's a list of women least likely and most likely to hump on the first night:

- Low Percentile Group:

Completely gorgeous girls, Asian women, girls in large groups, good face/big-titted women, girls dressed extremely sexily, chicks who'll dance but make little eye contact on the dance floor, teetotalers, girls with crosses on chains, a girl carrying the Jehovah's Witness newsletter "Awake" under her arm, South-African Caucasian women, girls better looking than you, cliquish women, insecure women, girls who know the bouncers, great dancers, very tall women, girls dancing with a different guy on every song and girls with lots of zits.

- Medium Percentile Group:

Ugly and/or fat girls, women with braces (on the teeth), women with hair past the ass, women wearing sneakers, big-titted women, sorority girls, shitty dancers and girls with mosquito bites for tits.

- High Percentile Group:

Above-average looking women, small/medium breasted chicks, short blond women (if you're a tall male), girls who talk to you first, drunk women, women in pairs (the better looking one of the two), women who go to the bar alone (rare), chicks who use the male john when the female side is too crowded, black women, slightly chunky brunettes sitting at the bar, out-of-town chicks whooping it up, the quiet friend of a loud, aggressive woman, women with over four earrings in one ear, a chick who'll do a shot with you, girls secure with themselves, extra-long-nailed women and chicks playing pool who yell "Hey sailor, buy me a drink!" at you when you're strolling to the pisser.

- Sure Things

Women who ask you to dance, a short blond who springs for a shot, any woman who mentions the word "cock" in conversation, a girl who asks what time's your class in the morning, and women who mention their nipple, naval and/or labial rings.

Two clarifications: fat and/or ugly girls are not high percentile because they're more than aware any attention they receive is only a desperate effort to get laid. If you yourself are fat and/or ugly enough so they opine you might still be there in the morning, their status automatically bumps to high percentile. And finally, girls with poor complexions are considered low percentile because they're concerned a whitehead may erupt during the make-out process, spraying zit juice in your eye.

21

Professors don't want you to know this, but their grading system usually works as follows: The people in the first two rows get the "A"s, those in rows three through nine pick up the "B"s, and the other folks get slapped with the rest of the letters in the alphabet.

Hard to believe but true. It would seem this little tip could get most anyone a 4.0 average with precious little effort. But it's not as easy as that. Complex sociological forces are at play here. See, from day one, each student is fatefully drawn to his slot in this classroom hierarchy by a necessary destiny. It seems a certain comfort level accompanies front, mid and back rowers. Displaced students interrupt a natural order, and usually suffer serious consequences.

Skeptics need simply witness a typical male back row guinea pig who's placed front and center. Results are loosely as follows: Upon being seated, the fellow's first impression is the piss-poor scenery. The only girls in sight are the bookish Plain Janes who still require a 90-degree swivel of the head. Plain Janes who, unlike the girls in the back, have little interest in playing eye-contact games for the next hour. The slouched posture and craning of the neck in search of a true babe divulges a misfit's presence, and, with the balance slightly out of kilter, stirrings in different pockets of the classroom occur. Soon, the entire front row senses something's amiss. The air reeks of a jackal at a lamb convention. These studious sorts fidget nervously in the presence of a rogue. The professor becomes attuned, and shoots dirty looks at the guy trying to screw with his grading system. Then he cruelly calls on the unlucky sort during lecture. Now, if a typical back rower is called on, the answers range from just wrong to laughable, with any correct answers attributed to luck and not much else. Front rowers, however, wear the cap of elevated expectation, and displaced back rowers simply aren't up to the task. So the experience is not just humbling, but an outright assault on the imposter's self esteem. A few reminders of a month's worth of blown-off readings produces the required humiliation to ensure he'll be 20 rows back by the next class, where he should have been in the first place.

A front rower relegated to the rear due to full-capacity seating undergoes the same fish-out-of-water experience. But for this soul, it's more like being in the wrong part of town after dark. The wallet gets moved to the front pocket, with the large bills slipped in a sock. This is the land of crib sheets and reverie. The stench of too much whiskey and beer from the previous night emanates from his neighbors' pores. The back-rowed front rower sometimes adopts mannerisms to fit in, attempting a cool, less conspicuous look. He reclines in his chair; if he's chewing gum, he pops it. He doodles above his notes, feigning boredom. He adjusts his watch so it doesn't beep at the top of the hour. Yet when the professor calls on him, his precise, articulate answer usually blows all covers.

Possibly the most irritating thing that can occur in class is the multi-sneeze/bless-you routine. It goes like this: Someone rips a sneeze, and a do-gooder from across the room remarks, "Bless you." The sneezer has no choice but to thank the person, although he's not quite sure what for. The sneezer then fires another, eliciting another "Bless you," and its successive thanks. The sneezer is just getting started however, and lets four more rip. The do-gooder, on a grand mission, blesses every one of the goddamned kerchews while the professor meanwhile is trying to lecture through it all. The sneezer becomes torn whether to continue thanking the asshole, causing an even *greater* disturbance, or to conspicuously cut him off altogether. It's a maddening exchange.

But these are the kinds of things the bored, restless mind focuses on during the low level, attendance-taking classes you have to slog through before you can take the good stuff. It's not unlike 15 years prior, when your parents dragged you to church and you had to construct a medley of amusements with minimal materials at hand.

Reducing the suffering of these classes is generally achieved in two ways—by 1) ignoring the professor entirely, or 2) using quirks in his personality to entertain yourself.

Ignoring the professor entirely is best achieved in the back row, where it's virtually impossible for him to hear or see your Walkman. If you forget your Walkman, daydreaming is a suitable fallback. Daydreaming requires slightly more effort than clicking on a Walkman, but luckily, tedious and irrelevant lectures naturally and quickly engage the mind into this mode.

An animated, quirky professor attempting to inject vitality into a dreary low-level class probably deserves your attention, but more as a prop rather than a source of information. Peripherals are what's key here. Notice the way his jaw flaps when he speaks, like a stoned person might do. Obsessively make note of any lateral movements. Be aware of the weird construction of the lecturer's ears, and all ears for that matter. Be careful where you go with this, however. Last semester I had a professor who shot his tongue out every few sentences to wet his lips—my bored-ass mental state decided it looked exactly like a frog snatching a fly out of the air. It messed with my mind. For the rest of the semester, I couldn't concentrate on a single thing the creature was saying.

Bring your lunch to these things. Get eating out of the way. Bring a magazine. Write a letter. See if the girl in front of you wants to engage in playing games with her chair, where you graze its flexible back with your knees to see if she'll lean back in acknowledgement. Remember, she's busy seeking relief from the same chronic boredom.

    You'd think one could just curl up and snooze through all this, but it's not that easy. For the desk situation in the classroom is bizarre. Some desks are actually built humanely and proportionately. But most, especially in lecture halls, have dimensions equivalent to the very ones found in a sixth-grade classroom. Someone somehow goofed and contracted grammar-school engineers to design college furniture. The desk is restrictive and uncomfortable for an average-sized person; for a tall sort it's almost claustrophobic. Taking notes is very nearly done in the fetal position. Some theorize that the design's intent *is* to discourage sleeping during lecture, since it's impossible for anyone but a yoga master to rest his or her head on the desk. If it's true, it's a failed concept; it only trains the student to adapt to sleeping upright. But mastering this method of sleeping usually takes a couple semesters.

22

An enduring college memory shall be the remarkable rip off that is the purchase of the textbook. The high price of textbooks most likely results from a clever scam orchestrated by a clandestine publisher/professor/bookstore-owner liaison. And that's my *least* paranoid thought on the subject. The scheme requires a five-foot stack of books for five classes (roughly a foot a class) charging already-broke students 12 times what each book is really worth. The inflated prices obligate the student to sell off the needed library at the end of the semester to help fund the following term's rip-off. The books now return about a ninth of their original cost; the store in turn resells them for about as much as they did the first time. Sometimes the books can't be sold back at all, because editions of algebra books, for example, are revised by the publisher every few years. This is to keep pace with the radical innovations occurring regularly in the field of algebra. But the bookstore hits the jackpot with books like The Grapes of Wrath, which, try as they might, the publishers can't revise and update. They'll change the cover a few times, calling it the 50th annual gold edition, etc., but that's the extent of it.

These publications the bookstore can resell endlessly, making hundreds of thousands of dollars on a measly $7.99 paperback.

But I'm jumping the gun. Because before the books are purchased, one must register for classes. Class scheduling is fairly simple. Monday, Wednesday and Friday classes as a rule are never scheduled before 10:00 a.m., to accommodate the Friday-morning hangover. Thursday night, remember, is as an important party night as Friday and Saturday in college. Sometimes better, when factoring in drink specials. Tuesday and Thursday classes can possibly be slotted as early as 9:00 a.m., but realize many more classes will be blown off at such an hour. The mind is very logical when it wakens too early, and assumes (correctly), "Why attend class when I can roll over and snooze some more?" Dreaded 8:00 o'clock classes are designed strictly for masochists, teetotalers, born-again Christians and oblivious freshmen. It seems most would avoid this time slot based on that demographic alone.

Classes are to be scheduled two or three hours apart. This is mandatory. Before explanations, some definitions are in order. Any hours in-between scheduled classes are considered "sandwiched." The last class of the day is termed "open ended." Sandwiched hours are the only periods of the day an AOPer can count on to study. Since another class looms in the distance, it's extremely difficult to devise a reason to blow off studying during the sandwiched hours in search of something less constructive. The future class somehow keeps the hedonistic thought processes at bay. Now, a blow off of studying of course isn't *impossible*. But it takes an extra-committed blow off, entailing blowing off all studying *and* the upcoming class or classes as well.

If one's schedule is constructed so classes are packed one after another, i.e. free from sandwiched hours, little choice is left but to try and study after the open-ended class. That's a script begging for disaster. I've tried it: you hit the library, open the book and the notes, sit there for a half hour thinking about the Asian babe in your psychology class, then close shop and go home. And the only time this won't occur is the day before a test, or during finals week.

Pseudo-sandwiched hours, incidentally, occur when you've got the first class of the day scheduled at 11:00 a.m., and you plan to arrive on campus at 9:00 a.m. "to study." The two hours in-between are pseudo-sandwiched hours. One may conclude such hours are as effective for studying as actual sandwich hours. The thing is this: if you have the discipline and concentration to get to campus a full two hours before your first class, you've probably got the willpower to study after an open-ended class or even God forbid in the evening or on weekends. And if *that's* somehow the case, you might as well just sleep in. That's why they're pseudo.

During the sandwiched hours, it's best to find a quiet table in the library on which to spread your belongings. Beware of the study cubicles. These devices serve primarily to even out any losses of sleep, rather than to actually study. They were created with good intentions, with the three walls functioning like blinders on a horse to produce distraction-free study environs. But their design is faulty. The walls are in such close proximity to the face, that trace amounts of carbon dioxide get inhaled in the stalls, slightly decreasing the oxygen level in the blood stream. The effect causes the eyes within minutes to slam shut, whereas a three-inch puddle of drool collects on the book.

Actually, naps as these are quite necessary for the college student, whose sleep patterns are erratic at best. Most students are nocturnal, and often function on minimal rest. They're in fact not dissimilar to another night creature, the feline. House cats take regular catnaps throughout the day to refresh themselves. Any moment the animal is free from obligation or commitment is spent taking a quick snooze. Students engage in similar rests, but in a less voluntary manner. These usually occur against their will, during a vital lecture or amid a pre-test study session. But the purpose is served none-the-less.

The involuntary nap is a scrappy little occurrence. It's no relation to actual sleep, with the enjoyable REM stages and relaxations. The nap exists rebelliously, wantonly, entrenched in a constant battle with the keepers of the conscious state. When it does prevail, it's usually short-lived. In sometimes less than a minute the mind mobilizes reinforcements, storms in and breaks up the party.

One of the most horrific things imaginable can occur in this half sleeping, half- waking state of limbo. To illustrate, it's best to start from the beginning. You get home at 3:00 a.m. from Washington's Pub, and set the alarm for 9:30 to attain maximum sleep hours before the 10:00 o'clock class. The alarm wails, and after one-too-many hits of the snooze button the clothes are donned and out the door you fly, foregoing breakfast and the pre-class crap. You hop on the bike, get to campus, and slalom at tremendous speeds through the people, pretending they're orange cones. It pisses them off to no end. You get to class at 10:05, which ain't bad considering the circumstances. Your physical state at this stage is wired from the hyped-up activity and remarkably geared for the lecture. The mind and body are pretty much in sync at this point, and both contribute to some bleary yet effective note taking.

But the class is long, and after 40 minutes, the body has cooled down, and now advises curling up to catch up on all that lost sleep. This of course rankles the mind, which is obediently trying to discover the ins and outs about Martin Heidegger. A minor struggle ensues. The mind shifts the lazy-ass body around in the chair, fidgets with its extremities, etc., but to no avail. In minutes the eyelids gently bounce off each other, finally coming to rest. The nap has arrived. It's not sleep, because certain cognizances are present. For one thing, the mind is still suspending the body in its upright state, proving it's at least partially in control. And the submerged mental state is somewhat attuned to respond to variances in environment, especially words along the lines of, "That wraps it up, class." In fact the nap's demise occurs the very moment it gets greedy and tries to evolve into sleep, allowing the body to succumb to gravity.

The mind knows this is unacceptable behavior in class, because the body crumples in a heap and loud, raspy snoring occurs. Luckily, the few scraps of consciousness left usually key in on this physical degeneration, and jerk the body awake. The concession to the nap appears to be contingent on its surreptitiousness, and an array of environmental alarm clocks are set to engage the waking state once it becomes anything but.

Meanwhile, the gut is gurgling from the 10 beers and late night nachos downed the night before, plus of course the lack of the morning shit. The rapid bike ride to class has caused a very nasty concoction to speedily snake its way through the small intestine and spill into the large bowel, where it's now on the downhill slope making demands to see daylight again in its metamorphosed state. And accompanying this mess is its equally hideous sidekick, known as the beer fart. The beer fart is of only moderate smell, really more bark than bite, but packs perhaps a greater perseverance to escape than the common fart. This isn't evident on weekends following partying, because the fart gets ripped the moment it's created, with little thought involved. In class, however, it's generally politely held. Problematically, 10 or 12 suppressed farts create a high-pressure gut, creating a dilemma. At this point, squeezing one relieves pressures, but, alas, now the chance of an inaudible creation is slight. Imagine trying to slip air out of the neck of a gigantic party balloon. It's exactly the same thing. So cutting one in advanced stages becomes unthinkable.

Consider the classroom nap amid this gurgling, pressurized state. Now, during the nap, the same socialization instinct that keeps the body upright suppresses the fart, and usually reliably so. But in certain instances, the body can prevail. Hiccupping, puking, sneezing, are all general examples of the body out willing the mind. Tragically, a wayward beer fart during a classroom nap is another. But in half consciousness, the catastrophe is never fully realized. There's even the possibility the sound and sensation wasn't a fart at all. Everything perhaps imagined? A neighbor putting his foot on your chair as another drops a book, creating a fart-like sensation/tonality, that fools the subconscious state?

Truth be told, the more likely scenario is this: you've just released a half-second vibratoed gasser breaking the somber silence of the lecture hall. One that by reasonable calculation reverberated at least as far as the professor. One that either aptly punctuated her sentence, or rudely interjected. It's a situation impossible to put a handle on. The whole matter becomes Kafkaesque. You're like a drugged, innocent bystander witnessing his own execution, incapable of defending himself for what he may or may not have done. All that's left to do is the detective game. You raise your now very-awake head, and take a big, reluctant whiff of air. Passing the scent test, the neighbors are checked for clues. No eye contact from three of them, but the chick to the left is looking and smiling. Or maybe she's just interested in me?? It's obviously a painful, joyless situation. The upside, if there *is* an upside, is that the experience ensures you'll stay wide-awake for the remainder of the class, as well as for the next full week of classes. It's that terrifying.

23

Tyce got arrested twice on his 21st birthday. And, admirably, they were two separate incidents. It's a stunt that may find no equal in the quiet town of Fort Collins. Tyce, however, always modest about his accomplishments, never made a big deal over it, perhaps a bit naive of its magnitude. Don and I, who aided and abetted the second arrest, were unable to witness the first time he got hauled in. But Tyce's story was a gem. And nearly unbelievable.

Tyce got into Washington's saloon with a fake ID (he turned 21 at midnight). After closing, his drunken buddy was tooling home by means of a one-way street going the wrong way. The cops who do laps around the bars waiting for idiocy to reveal itself immediately pulled the guy over.

"Didn't you see the arrow?" the cop stoically asked.

"Arrow? I didn't even see the Indian," Tyce swears his buddy replied. As the cop started to haul the guy away, he noticed a beer pitcher in the back seat that Tyce had clipped from the bar. "Where'd that come from?" Tyce, sporting the philosophy that an honest man has nothing to fear, confided the truth. So the cop obligingly handcuffed Tyce, stuffing him in the squad car as well. I think Tyce saw all of his buddies getting arrested with such regularity that maybe a side of him felt left out. It created a kind of void in him, an incompleteness. The bastard cops were purposefully neglecting him. But he made up for these oversights, pronto.

Tyce was released in the early morning on his own recognizance, and hoofed it back to the dorms before dawn. I let the poor bastard sleep in till 9:00 a.m., then balanced a heaping shot of rot-gut whiskey to his side of the suite and woke him with the scent. "Happy birthday motherfucker!!" He reluctantly obliged, cursing me, and I joined him, shuddering. People don't have 21st birthdays very often, and we were determined to make this one memorable. We roused Don the same way, grabbed a small bag of weed and zoomed off for Louie's Liquors.

The proprietor arrived at the same time we did, and unlocked the joint. We looked around at the empty world before us: it was vacant—no cars, no people anywhere—only the liquor man. He was a bird-like, odd-looking little fellow whose craggy exterior betrayed a hard, dues-paying life—he likely had to quit the juice years ago 'cause it was ruining him—and now with his wife gone and kids repossessed he was surrounded by this potion that alone embodies all that is divine and evil in the world—the yin and the yang 'cept he's just yinning these days, with a bottle of yang six inches from his nose. How long can he hold out? In my electric hungover head where anything's possible I felt deep sorrow for his plight. How many more like him? I wanted to portray a world not so onerous, to offer to stock the guy's shelves or dust his counters. I wanted to prove deeds of good still exist in the severe world, that even wounded hope has wings.

Diverting the focus, Tyce bellowed, "What in fuck do we want, tequila or whiskey?" I gently asked our shop owner the prices of the respective pints behind the counter, so as not to rattle him any further.

"Six-fifty for the whiskey, $6.10 for the tequila," he squeaked. His voice was whiny and discomfiting. It blew the whole mood. I at once lost all sympathy for the scrawny nitwit. So we busted out of the store, having decided on the whiskey. We were going to be the town bums today, and whiskey is more bum-like. Outside, still a ghost town. We felt like challenging the haggard world with fists flying. Hell, why not a doubled-backed line at the liquor store or something? Why not a freakin' parade, a spontaneous street party, a quick evacuation of the slow-burning houses? Why not just one other goddamned soul with a plan as heavenly and demonic as ours? Eighteen billion people perched on the earth and we were alone in our revelry. What's wrong with this pitiful excuse of a college town? Where were the others searching for the lost question, the fateful answer, the mystery door with the steaming pile of shit on the other side, waiting to be stepped in??

We drove about three blocks and then parked, choosing to saunter into downtown like a derelict posse. Bums don't motor about, looking for parking spaces. A large paper grocery bag was intended to disguise the booze, but every time we swilled, the huge brown flag waved to the passing souls, demanding public attention. We became buzzed after just a few swigs 'cause we hadn't eaten anything. Tyce spotted a delivery truck with baked muffins, etc. with the back door open. We stealthily grabbed a bunch of rolls and chowed them down. It seemed appropriate at the time to hurl the leftover buns at the cars rolling by. We marauded the local Safeway, pocketing various sundries. Someone needed smokes—we hit the liquor store on College Avenue where they don't keep the pints behind the counter and pocketed more whiskey.

To complete the theme, we scoped for alleys to drink in—broken-glass urine-smell alleys with last night's bedroll in a heap by the dumpster—where graffiti and vomit-stained walls are raised high, keeping the sun out—sad streets corralled out of sight and mind from respectable America—but tragically, downtown Fort Collins in all its decency had nothing of the kind to offer. So we found the coldest, hardest piece of concrete available behind a shopping center and made do with it. Our stomachs now lined with food accepted the drink more agreeably, and all mild hangovers melded with the present buzz. Once comfortable in our element, we began crudely complimenting the pretty female shoppers shuffling forth. "Whadja buy me, beautiful?" We used hoarse, weathered voices. But our look was far too collegiate middle-class to arise any true offenses. The shoppers dismantled the ruse in the split second it took to pass on by. It pissed us the hell off. We counted on enduring all that was insolent, needful and pitiful; those choices were made clearly unavailable. We were insultingly branded with labels of expectation and achievement.

"Maybe they'll take us seriously 50 years down the road," Tyce commented. "'Cause I ain't leaving."

And he practically moved in, until late afternoon when we got hungry. So we took off and stumbled through downtown on narrower sidewalks searching for food. Tyce was starting to lag; Don and I had 50 paces on him. We wheeled around and saw him sauntering forth, pants and undies dropped to his ankles. He walked proudly, chin held high, oblivious to the small scene he was creating. His pubic hair rustled in the breeze. It was some last-ditch effort before his final return to civilization. We reached our original starting point, the Safeway parking lot, having made a large lap around town. We balanced precariously on the huge concrete expanse; the Colorado sun beat down upon us. Birds playfully bathed in puddles in the parking lot.

The serenity of the moment however was interrupted when three squad cars came blazing forth from different directions, "surrounding" us. In the cops' interrogation they seem more interested in the cowboy-hatted Tyce, and kept saying to him, "We know what you did, you may as well admit it." Our hazy heads were struggling to recall. Lessee, there were the buns ripped-off before they were flung at the cars, there was the stolen whiskey; couldn't convincingly argue the public drunkenness issue and meanwhile they began frisking us to find a bevy of unopened toiletries including toothpaste, Visine, Certs, whiskey, razors, etc. plus of course my bag of weed. Finally a cop spared us our faulty sense of recall and mentioned the one offense no one considered—some old hag reported Tyce dropping his drawers, describing him to a tee. They took us all in, I guess Don too as an accomplice or something. A cop was cool to me, however, and tossed the weed down the john as I watched on. Tyce was the only one booked, on an indecent exposure misdemeanor. The cop also gave him this five-minute paternal lecture after discovering he was arrested 15 hours before, concluding with, "This is no way to begin your adult life, young man." Tyce heard not a word, only lamenting on the way out, "That bastard'll sober ya up." Indeed, he did us all.

24

In four-plus years of college with all the carousing, drinking, and partaking of illegal substances, getting arrested is an inevitability. Cops only arrest college students on these charges: public intoxication, disorderly conduct, interference, DUI, pissing in public, drug possession, indecent exposure, and shoplifting/dining-and-dashing. By a poor stroke of luck, all college kicks fit into one of these categories. When your time comes, AOP recommends heartily kissing the district attorney's ass at the arraignment. She often has some leeway to lessen the charge and keep it out of court. Flaunt your college status and reveal earnestness of your schooling—borrow a calculus book to take with you. A semester or two of drama classes can really pay off at this point. To illustrate, once I dined and dashed with a novice who kept ordering dish after dish—about 12 fuckin' courses—the drunken idiot arose so much suspicion that after we darted a block away for the van, the cops were summoned and we were pulled over in seconds. My buddy went to court before me, pled guilty, and split for the summer. I got out the old monkey suit, dusted off and donned the glasses and explained to the attractive district attorney we thought we had left a 20 and a one on the table instead of two ones. She ate this right up from the upstanding college student and recommended the judge drop the charge. But this kind of luck is rare; court is a more likely outcome. If such is the case, always plead innocent, rehearse your bullshit well, and stay in the night before (avoiding beer breath).

Cops are not to be buddied with—their sole intent is to destroy your good time. It may be necessary to initially throw the "sirs" around in attempts to avoid an arrest/ticket; if that doesn't work, doubly curse the fucker for allowing you to humiliate yourself. Never ever admit anything to a cop, and never trust a cop. Once an officer in a cruiser saw me from the back pissing in an alley against a Dumpster—I foolishly admitted the trivial act, assuming the cop would respect my honesty, realizing the harmlessness of the situation. The bastard wrote me a ticket. When I told the district attorney I'd easily whip it in court since the cop never technically witnessed the act she said yeah, but it says here you admitted it. I screwed myself by being honest to a cop, mistakenly assuming the sonuvabitch was human.

Law enforcement varies geographically. Generally, the smaller the city, the more fucked-up the cop. The only places where cops are tolerable are huge cities, which provide a normal context for law and order. In such places, law enforcement is applied to real crime, like burglaries, shootings and muggings. A city cop witnessing a dog off a leash in a park won't even blink. The big city sees laws enforced with intelligence, not simply because they're on the books.

Small town cops' priorities are reversed. While few real criminal acts exist, they remain as busy as their urban brethren by upgrading all petty violations. And these are rigidly enforced, in serious fashion. An open container of beer at a lake is sufficient cause to radio in backups. The mindset is much more mechanical, assuming if a law exists, it damn well needs enforcing.

Cops break up parties because AOP-land democracy works like this: if 3500 people are whooping it up at a party in collective peak experience, and one old lady a block away gets pissed off and calls the cops, and they take a vote and it's 3500 to one, the old coot wins in a landslide and the party's over. It's based on the little-known statute stating that lifeless, rule-loving simpletons have the most power in our country, and irresponsible, kicks-loving sorts have the least. Fun regulation is easy to understand. When someone notices you're having fun and they're not, they immediately despise you for it. At that point they're having even *less* fun, and it's all because of you. They figure if your fun level can somehow be reduced, theirs will logically increase inversely. But it only works in theory.

If the cop breaking up the party is civil to you, he certainly should be shown basic respect. But what really eats me up is watching otherwise intelligent college students kowtow to a tough-shit cop. Most bully cops are like fifth-grade bullies—they back down when challenged. They're so accustomed to people blindly accepting their "authority," they're taken aback and fold when someone doesn't.

It's always been my twisted impression anyway that since *I'm* paying these guys' salaries, I should be telling *them* what to do. And being public servants, their first concern oughtta be scurrying around, ensuring everybody at the bash has at least one drink in their hands. But most cops will draw the line at this, because their role of public servant has evolved over time. Their position originally required managing and mediating tenuous situations in the community with fairness, compromise and empathy, employing an acute understanding of sociological and societal complexities to better complete their mission. Detaining those who threatened the social order became an occasional necessity, all in an effort to create and maintain a safe and livable community.

Over the years, that function has been fine-tuned and adjusted; most cops now are simply menacing, revenue-collecting dupes. Especially the ones in sleepy college towns. Strict imposers of the fun tax. This isn't overly evident to those holed up with a stack of videos on a Friday night. But if an excess of joy coupled with traces of offbeat amusement is publicly displayed, especially with abandon, it's certain a law-enforcement officer somewhere will work overtime to rid it away.

Fort Collins cops have discovered a way to quell kicks and collect revenue in one fell swoop by making eternal laps around the bar district, breaking only to gas up and rotate shifts. This makes everyone caught in the fervent cause to eradicate drunk driving sleep a bit easier. This extra-lucrative form of revenue collecting is cleverly tangled in the inviolable web of morality and safety, so its monstrous, ingenious campaign exists virtually without challenge. The wily sponsors simply shamelessly sport pictures or videos of a young crash-victim skipping rope, and walah!—enforcement is tripled and DUI fines are raised enough to buy a new fleet of cop cars by winter. Of course, the symptom rather than the problem is quite intentionally addressed. And that's because solutions like establishing alternate transportation, etc. would eliminate the reward of big revenues. True abolition of drunk driving would starve the system, so its perpetuation coupled with great moral indignation remains the norm.

But drunk-driving issues are old hat. These days, a related phenomenon is what chiefly rankles AOP: the enactment of For-Your-Own-Good (FYOG) laws. As we speak, some do-gooder somewhere is proudly implementing a FYOG law. It's a boom time for this stripe of law and order in the Land of the Free and the Home of the Terminally Blah.

A FYOG law is generally created by a simpleton who, with missionary fervor, attempts to spread dulldom to all corners of the earth. Seatbelt laws, helmet laws, no- smoking-in-bar laws, curfews-for-people-under-18 laws, sobriety and/or seatbelt checkpoints—the list doubles daily, and the kick is that the public eats up such impositions without debate, convinced their own good is indeed being serviced. In fact, inherent in these laws is the implication that all challengers either have something to hide or are morally suspect.

Safety laws are FYOG laws, and are perhaps the hardest to stomach. What could be more insulting than an adult getting a ticket for jeopardizing his or her own safety? AOP is quite aware of the undercurrent of intention in this new wave of moral legislation. Safety and kicks are polar opposites, incompatibles—when complete Safety is present, Kicks must leave the building. Something was needed to replace the flagging sale of the consequence of sin; Safety has bravely resuscitated this antiquated concept and has assumed the New Morality. And the end results are equally effective.

Safety laws replicate so quickly and dangerously because they're difficult to counter. They are initiated by seemingly "caring" individuals or organizations, and tender supporting arguments that are (superficially) infallible. In reality, their supporters are sick proselytizers, pitiful plebs who, under this guise of public concern, desire even more converts to their narrow, rule-filled lives. And now armed with actual laws on their side, they can tangibly punish their dissenters. So it's the goal of these modern-day missionaries, this wretched colony of TV addicts, to either convert or crush all souls desiring to live their lives relatively freely. It's assumed that any individuals venturing below the surface of the tepid, piss-filled water in which they're treading is either in critical need of rescuing or a good drowning.

It's difficult not being bothered by such trash. How to describe to the uninitiated the beauty and sheer necessity of danger and unpredictability—flying on a motorcycle at unearthly speeds with all senses fully engaged, rendering the rider more aware and alive than ever before—how to explain the obvious irony? The closer one dances towards death the larger life becomes, and many of life's meanings are offered on these hallowed, fragile grounds. Their search becomes effortless—-they'll humbly come knocking on the door.

Not including all the ones in-between, it seems two diametrically opposed mindsets roam this land, referred to here as Group "Z" and Group "A."

The overwhelming majority resides in Group "Z." "Z" accepts the unruffled world before him and necessarily provides the backbone of society. He and his cronies define the status quo. "Z" upholds most traditions and customs of the culture, and half-consciously perpetuates them. Life in Group "Z" isn't overly stimulating or exciting, but it ain't half bad. Friends for one thing abound—it takes little effort to find like-minded folk around. And that's important, because "Z"'s moderate satisfactions are usually dependent on social acceptance—with "success" being dictated by an external standard. Sources of enjoyment, entertainment, are plentiful for "Z," with such things neatly packaged by the culture: television sports, sit coms, action movies, bingo, etc. "Z" also subscribes to the dominant religion of the culture, which answers all the philosophical, heady questions that may arise when sickness and death occur.

Group "A" is from some other planet. Planet AOP. The societal prescriptions for enjoyment only induce disease for "A." "A" has atypical appetites, and gets bored real easily if they aren't fed. "A" will try it all in life—extreme sports, drink and drugs, travel, a myriad of sexual partners—continuing in a circular quest. "A" is often a loner, as his standard for fulfillment is more personalized, internalized. Fringe behavior provides the quick fix of contentment, but, entrapped in the great equilibrium factory that is the human body, emotional lows can ride with the highs. Satisfactions are temporary, and often result in the stakes simply being raised.

"A"'s "aberrance" snowballs. He or she finds that once certain icons are removed, the whole stockpile comes tumbling down. Attempts to answer an offbeat inner voice spawn hundreds of new questions. Problems in accepting customary points of view result, and a self-imposed exile from the mainstream is often created.

A rickety bridge connects these personality types. "Z" people logically see no redeeming value in purposely risking the physical vehicle that harnesses their mind, their entire *being* on the planet. They value life enough not to be playing any foolish games that might snuff or impair it. Such irresponsibility extends far beyond individual selfishness, as it affects family members, friends and loved ones. It's foolhardy, self- indulgent and often immoral behavior.

"A" people, conversely, cannot abide an existence under a turtle's shell. They believe disrobing the irrational fear of inevitable death is a necessary step towards fulfillment. Existence is far more qualitative than quantitative for these sorts, and risk taking is inherent in their enjoyments. The fears that do exist are only those of a common, meaningless life. "A" thinks the sad majority is too timid to find its true calling, which surely must dissent with the impartations of mass-ordered civilization. True sin to "A" is this: after winning the impossible lottery of birth, squandering the whole thing on a passive, waveless existence occupied with rote tasks. If God does exist says "A," would He not desire that we author and celebrate a unique, fulfilling and glorious life?

A peaceful coexistence could be had if "Z" didn't feel the need to drown "A" in a sea of statutes and ordinances. But 'tis the ongoing commitment of a majority begging and drooling for even more regulation. Call it of couch potato McCarthyism. Call it the weed-eater patrol. Whatever it's called, is it any wonder that it's produced a small hoard of antithetical rejects like those in AOP land? And is it surprising that these malcontents work overtime trying to flip off the system?

Actually, "Z"ish sensibilities don't end there. They're safely applied across the board, to all levels of the human experience. Forays into the twisted depths and darknesses of the human psyche are quickly resolved by "Z" experts, dubbed legislatively and tucked neatly away. If a kid goes to school and shoots up the class, 12 shrinks from the Federal Assembly to Solve Child Fuck-ups will concur that 1000 grams of vitamin B 12 in kids' diets combined with metal detectors in all schools would avert such tragedies. If a toddler is run over on the sidewalk, the mother successfully passes a law requiring all cars to slow to five mph when a baby stroller is in view. All that is inherently savage, irrational and unpredictable in nature are considered system glitches by the authorities, eradicable with a modicum of fine-tuning.

It's a celebration of the dullards, and yet another triumph of good over evil. It's a pat on the back, a reassurance; it's the one bright, shining lie we're too happy to hear. And all a pathetic attempt to gloss over what we don't understand, and to hide from the fact that a skin layer away from this sterile womb we've created is a chaotic, twitching reality waiting to rear its ugly head.

Let AOP be a homage, a paean to such disorder. Call it an ode to the darkness, a greasy proposition of the unwelcome truth. With clammy, shaking hands, of course.

25

Money in college is so scarce it's ridiculous. There are simply too many students and not enough greenbacks to go around. All these smiling people strolling about campus, sporting nice clothes, attending fine classes, are in reality living in abject poverty. Campus is like a huge slum that's neatly and ingeniously disguised. The difference between the moneyless college student and the moneyless non-college student, however, is huge. Your date in school would be fine celebrating her birthday dinner at Burger King; the non-college date conversely would hit the ceiling in this instance. College is perhaps the only time in one's life when the huge societal value of having money has little bearing. So, while students only have as little in their pockets as the beggar on the street, they're not psychologically ruined by it. That doesn't occur until a few years following graduation. Actually, being nearly indigent contributes to the challenge of college life. It spices it up. One learns to appreciate more with less. And when a windfall does occur, it's all the more reason to celebrate.

One early spring Saturday, Tyce received such a surprise. It was a tax refund for $48.67, an exorbitant lump of money by any college standard. The money was to be spent all at once he reasoned, for maximum enjoyment. We raced for the car to make the bank while it was still open, then gassed it for Louie's Liquors.

We roared into Louie's parking lot and jumped out. We were both feeling giddy with fortune. Just an hour before, I was hungoverly figuring ways to devise a day of kicks on two minutes of money ($3.80). Tyce lifted his nose high, and focused it towards the store. "I believe I can smell whiskey in the air," he announced. He ambled forth, intentionally assembling a look of newfound importance. Louie, the storeowner, took us for just a couple more cheap-ass students. We'd predictably head to the student section of the store, where the $3.99 twelvers and the rotgut whiskey resided. Imagine his surprise when we high falutinly strolled past the Shaeffer, beyond the Old Milwaukee and straight to the microbrew section. He put down the paper and straightened up, realizing perhaps he had some *real* customers. For us it was like living a dream: the whiskey we browsed for was at eye level rather than shoelace level. The chaser soda was strictly name brand. We ended up buying $45 worth of beer and booze, with two bucks left for two fat-cat cigars.

Tyce received a quarter in change. His wealth lasted just shy of an hour. Unburdened, he could now resume his old ways—broke and happy.

We went to the dorm room, and put down a few. Tyce was donning his cowboy hat. He became energized from the whiskey and perched on the edge of the chair, ready to leap off at any given excuse. The talk, as always, was of women. I asked Tyce if he could ever be happy settling down with just one.

"No doubt bro. In fact I'm positive at some time during this crazy search I'll stumble on the ultimate woman—a little beauty inside and out who'll make me consider no other. And I'm gonna return to her night after night, no matter how many sweeties try and lure me away."

The comment put him in a new light. "Wow. That's damn commendable," I said and meant. "Complete fidelity. Imagine rejecting a pass from a young, olive-skinned nymphet with just-ripened breasts and a 17-year-old ass out of sheer commitment and devotion." I viewed the man with a heightened regard. It honestly made me a little misty. "My friend, that's beautiful," I said.

Tyce's expression changed. His idealisms were never churned through a rigorous test like *that*. Something wasn't processing correctly. Maybe I stuck one-too-many nymphet adjectives in there. He funneled the information into his brain over and over, and still received a faulty output, that of banging the doll on the pool table. He paused for a long moment, conflicted. "I might bend a bit on business trips," he compromised.

It was time for the pilgrimage to the CD stack. Proper choice of a CD could transform an ordinary day into a spiritual journey. We almost simultaneously agreed on Dire Straits' "Making Movies." Nothing was more appropriate for the moment.

Tyce retreated to the far corner of the room. He saddled up to the invisible Hammond organ and droned the carnivalesque introduction to the first song, "Tunnel of Love." He quickly abandoned such tinkerings as the song powered forth and switched to drums, solidly mapping out directions and providing the fuel to feed the song. His eyes were muscled shut in tight squint, his long torso slightly bent with arms flailing madly. He played to a corner of the room, where just beyond the walls were thousands of adoring teenage girls screaming in adulation, eyes fixed on Tyce alone. His elbows narrowed as he tossed out spontaneous drum rolls, then widened again as he kept time. He stomped the floor for added emphasis, head bobbing up and down in agreement, and made occasional collisions with the walls in front of him. The image conjured some gypsy dance with the music itself the leading partner, the two meshed in perfect synchronicity.

I took the opposite corner of the room. Guitar was my choice of instrument, though I chose to pick the notes rather than play fingerstyle like Knopfler. I'd also sing it for the little pretties that paid good money to see us. With the accompanying vocals yelling from behind, the only way of hearing your own was to sing three inches from the corner of the room, where the acoustics provided a self-microphone.

During the funky instrumental bridge we made a rare foray to the center of the pad. I scratched out a couple notes, then fired a rapid three-note pull-off. The band quieted for Tyce's answer—a funky back beat, punctuated with a triple roll. The call/response continued for a few bars, then the rest of the band leapt forth, shoving the rhythm section to the background once again.

"You sing circles around this guy," Tyce said.

"Thassright. And when I graduate I'm going to Cali to show the world how it's done. Stick with the keys mister; maybe we'll both tear it up out there."

But we had to first study our invisible chops here in 1111 at Westfall Hall. Strangely, few souls exist who can dorm-room jam with pure abandon. As if the tally of all their other worries somehow isn't enough, some can additionally fret over how they look playing an air guitar rapturously. And, unable to do it without anxiety, their finger points at the uninhibited, how they resemble idiots.

And idiots perhaps we were. But the air jam goes way beyond the tunes. Letting go is the crux of AOP. To master ripping the stinging eyes of the public off the back. Can any real joys be found amid the distressed, scrutinizing state of the so-called norm? Or does everything worthwhile begin with a giant step in the other direction?

Tyce broke out a joint. My instincts were to pass, since it would limit my sociability outside the room, but I felt like I owed him, since he supplied the booze and all. After smoking 3/4 of it we slipped on The Stones' Sticky Fingers, and things got funky. Every time Charlie Watts ended a sentence with a drum roll, Tyce drum rolled on the wall, causing books to fall off shelves. Our neighbor banged back; Tyce yelled, "Hey listen to the echo," and did it again. He was right: it echoed. He was in his corner, I in mine. I glanced around and did a double take;

Tyce's jeans were now to his ankles, and he was sporting boxers with red hearts. He was very diligently trying a dance with the right foot anchored by the restrictive jean situation, and the left foot pirouetting around awkwardly. Had he chalk on the left shoe, it would have sketched a full circle.

I wasn't convinced I couldn't do the shuffle a bit better. The jeans went south and I gave the protractor dance a try, adding an occasional rabbit-hop during the chorus. The jeans gave the sensation of ankle cuffs—had a fire broken out, we'd have been doomed to run in circles in our skivvies until we were reduced to charcoal.

Next, the door swung open. It was Tom, one of the nondescript guys from the east side of the floor. The thing is, when you're stoned and surprised, defenses instinctually arise. Slow motion best describes the scene that ensued:

Zero minute: Music cranked up to seven. I, Tyce, dancing madly, pants dropped to ankles. *Zero minute:* Door opens. It's Tom. *.5 seconds*: "Do you guys…" are the only three words from his mouth. *One second:* I, Tyce transform blissful, stoned looks to one of alarmed surprise. *1.9 to 3.6 seconds*: I, Tyce hastily yank up trousers, sustaining startled facial expressions. *1.9 to 3.6 seconds*: Tom's cheerful facial expression converts to one of horror. *3.6 to 5.6 seconds*: Absent explanation from the formerly pantsless idiots. *5.6 seconds:* Tom states "Never mind" and closes door.

When one is stoned and an incident of weight occurs, the mind initially keeps thinking, "Did that really happen?" And, sadly, there's no way of proving it did. But since Tyce's account of the recent past mirrored my own, we figured the said event most likely took place. And at that point it became the most comical thing imaginable. We'd never laughed so thoroughly. Peripheral laugh muscles atop the intestines received a year's workout. They were weak from lack of regular use, and struggled to support the activity. The laughter became painful, and our souls rose above the couch and actually observed two doubled-over units of flesh become helpless victims of the strangeness that is complete, irrepressible laughter.

We agreed to never explain or justify the situation to Tom. The poor fellow would have to reconcile it in whatever way he saw fit.

26

It was a Saturday around 11:00 p.m., and Wilt, an ex-frathead named Rick and I were cruising campus streets on our bicycles searching for a good, raucous bash. We happened upon a frat toga party which at that moment had eight gorgeous girls filing in, all clad in tight, sexy togas. It indicated we found our destination. We weren't averse to hitting frat parties despite the fact that lots of frat people were there; our delicate mission was to steal their women and drink their beer. We reached the door and what?? were denied entry! We were toga-less and considered outsiders! Miscreants! The door folk were unbending and practical: they couldn't even be swayed by offerings of whiskey. We racked our brains—where to get a toga at this hour? And so far from home? The images of the eight beauties a piss arc away wrested our minds into a private hell, as we pondered the bleak unfairness of the situation and of life in general. We shook it off and scurried down different pathways of thought. What would Plato do if he stumbled onto a coat-and-tie affair? We prayed to Dionysis, the coolest Greek god we knew for answers. Rick had already given in, and eyed the bikes in resignation.

Suddenly, Wilt began madly stripping off his clothes. Wilt is kind of a nudist at heart and attends nudist camps in the summer, but I didn't get the connection. I mentioned what-the-fuck but he didn't answer; he seemed determinedly on a mission. After his clothes were off, he tied the shirt around his waist and tossed his pants over one shoulder loincloth style. He paused with his underwear for a minute, and then looped it onto the other shoulder as an afterthought. Luckily it was devoid of skid marks. The getup was a fuckin' work of art. All this was too much for Rick, so he took off. I stripped and designed my own toga with my duds, and we valiantly marched to the door. The party guards let us in on drunken idiocy alone.

The place was bananas inside—it was truly like a Roman orgy—a vast swirl of energy with a loud band in the back making it so that when you spoke with a chick you had to get so close your lips would sensuously rub her cheek—again confirming the crazy knowledge that everything but everything you do is a mating ritual, even the way you fill her beer from the keg with unfaithful eyes now wrestling with that one over there for one, two, three seconds, sometimes a stare down that lasts days with the brave ones. And the girls squeezing past in the ever-tight quarters who offer a knowing backrub with their precious breasts—that unmistakable soft-firm feeling as you lean back a hair to acknowledge—and with it all the sad realization that these silent interactions, these subconscious seductions all shall be squandered with everyone aware of the newness of the night. Forever contending with the joy of the moment is the regret of what you could have had in this short perfect life with too many choices—but it clearly was too early to consider settling into any domestic eight-hour relationships.

AOPers can sense after one tour if the party's going to be worthwhile—this one was pounding with so much early energy it was certain to be another for the books. Wilt and I of course were wearing perfect conversation pieces, and Wilt picked up on the huge advantage and partook in another mission to talk to every last chick at the party—he just makes the rounds, says his thing, contorts his rubber face with the joy or agony of the moment and moves on—some are amused and entertained, while the tight-lipped sorority nannies who were taught to scoff do so, phasing him not one whit. By Wilt's senior year he met all 12,000 women on campus give or take a few; they'd yell out while driving past his sidekick sober-self on an afternoon stroll—who was that?—huh?—fuck if he knew.

I lost Wilt for an hour; I was discussing a sideways life with an upright sorority girl until her sisters rushed in and rescued her. I wended my way through the increasing hoards up the stairs and immediately noticed Wilt camped out in the barber's chair—it's an armchair that leans way back and an attendant pours alcohol down your throat until you signal, 'cept Wilt never signals and the guy panics and stops anyway. Wilt had discovered the ideal seating arrangement. The thing is, he was oblivious that his dick and balls were in full view as he sat wide legged in his idiot garb, and were the first three things all 800 people filing up the stairs witnessed. It seemed to contribute to the party's entertainment value, so I didn't break it to him.

Around 2 a.m. we had a chugging contest going with some frat boys who believed this is what partying's all about. Hopefully they were right, since Wilt and I placed one and two at the thing with the bastard barely winning 'cause he purposely verticaled early spilling a quarter of the beer—my competitive juices were flowing and I cried foul pointing to the soaked underwear draped around his shoulder—damning evidence indeed—but Willy wouldn't hear it—he responded with a three-second belch, reconfigured his ever-present grin and stumbled off, in tainted victory.

An hour later the bash was *still* jamming, but it was time to get serious—we hooked up with two girls we knew from the dorms—a tall, slim blonde named Stacy who always liked me and her chunkier friend with large breasts for Wilt—can't remember the name. The girls had moved off campus for the spring semester; we caravanned to their new house for a rousing game of strip poker. Chicks always have the upper hand in these games since they're usually donning earrings and necklaces, requiring many losses before having to remove the good stuff. Wilt and I looked a hand away from losing before even starting, with beer-dampened duds hanging in pathetic knots around our torsos.

Wilt lost the first game and tossed the pretzeled pants; after losing the second he forgot about the shoes and socks and off flew the shirt that was around his waist. The fellow was naked from the shins up before the first beer was downed. His underwear was apparently getting trampled in some room back at the party. Clad in just his sneakers, he looked poised for a nudist basketball game. The first loser in these games normally sits with the body parts you're allowed to display in public hiding the body parts you're supposed to keep hidden. Wilt bypassed this ritual, however, and casually lay on his back like he was soaking up rays by the pool. But in a half hour we all lost sufficiently, with the girls opting to retain their panties, a gentle violation of the game rules.

The amazing thing was that clothesless Stacy suddenly elevated from above average to gorgeous, at least body wise—the transformation was remarkable. It was like discovering a hidden gem. Wilt and I did numerous double takes. We discussed it with her for five full minutes, making her friend mull over plans to hit the gym.

"Your body is stunning."

"Yes it is, it's quite excellent."

"That stomach is a gift from heaven." Stacy ate up the commentary and purred like a kitten. The subject interested her—she went through lengths not to change it until all its levels were exhausted completely. She purposely made frequent saunters to the bathroom, kitchen and foyer, making her now-rival livid. After Stacy decided to check on the CDs across the room on the high shelf, Wilt's chick grabbed his hand

and heaved him into the bedroom. As their door clicked shut, I settled down with Stacy on a pillowed floor in front of a cold fireplace, taking a closer look, and we engaged in an enjoyable, mutually rewarding lovemaking session. She was a spectacular kisser, by the way.

27

The AOP gang played lots of poker games, and it was after one of these that I became victim to a weakness I'd never experienced. Great mountains of bad karma are sure to shadow me for the remainder of life. I committed perhaps the greatest of faux pases, at least in my eyes, plunging me into the rarely trodden world of true remorse.

Wilt, Mac, Darrell, Darrell's girlfriend Liz and her girlfriends were there; also Rick and Wilt's sister Mona. A round-table discussion somehow merged into a strip poker game, which lasted till around 3 a.m. After the game, we re-clothed, cranked the music and engaged in one final phase of partying, whereas the guests one by one toppled over, crashed on various parts of the floor. Soon I too was down for the count. Liz, perhaps by design, chose to sleep five feet away, with her boyfriend Darrell passed out in some corner.

Now if I've been partying and face sleeping alone on a weekend night, some instinct mandates a remedy—not necessarily a search for sex, but for at least a nice, warm body to play with and lie with. Four options were available. The northeast corner housed Cindy, also a journalism major; I even had a photography class with her. Assessment:

cute, the poker game revealed a darn good body, high receptivity level, but so damned *nice*, a move would be uncomfortable. She was a quiet, moral, fun-loving Colorado girl who associated sex with healthy, long-termed relationships. I didn't want to be the first to corrupt such a pristine vision. The circumstance would ensure we'd both be teeming with stress, anyway. One must take care not to damage another in life, and she seemed on the fragile side.

Katie was crashed over by the stereo—a long, thin body with full, large breasts, especially considering her thinness, a trait I always find a turn-on. Excellent receptivity level—she'd had it for me since day one in Westfall. *Huge* downside—I think she shaves above her lip. It's curious, but some months prior a bunch of us for some reason were playing spin-the-bottle, and when I planted a deep one on ol' Katie, I swear I felt something like razor stubble. My mouth said something like "very nice" but my mind let out a high-pitched scream. Her subconscious might even have heard it. I mean, take a semester off and save for electrolysis, *anything* for God's sake. Needless to say, the smooch cancelled all further activities for just a day under forever.

Laura, on the couch, bore a no-receptivity level. She was good-looking but not my type (nor I hers)—an insecure sorority girl who surrounds herself with like-minded friends, laughing and carrying on, always pretending their shit is tightly packed together. Laura's got inane conversation down to such an art, she's developed a way to rig all chats so no more than a 1/2 second can ever pass in horrid silence. She wasn't built for spontaneous immodesty anyway. When her bra finally came off during the game, she guarded her tits so cross-*armedly*, her nipples actually became cross-*eyed*. When it was her turn to deal she'd only relinquish one hand, so the process took like 20 minutes.

Lastly, of course, requiring no travel expenses whatsoever was Liz, right in front of my face. She was off limits, being with Darrell and all. Sure, they were experiencing problems, I mean Darrell was passed out way over near the *refrigerator*, but even the consideration was out of the question. Anyway, sleep herself was beginning a slow seduction until…about 5:00 o'clock, when I awoke to Liz's eyes beaming right into my bleary ones. I believe she willed mine open. For all I know, she was poised like that for two hours straight. It was a surreal moment: I was midway between the waking and crashed state, so all real occurrences could have been passed off as a dream and vice versa. In fact it turned out to be an interesting state of consciousness, allowing a convenient detachment from most normal responsibilities.

Christ, we didn't even screw, but Lord was she a fine kisser and gawd did she possess full, soft, fine Italian breasts. Instant 2:00 o'clock-boner-producing milk sacs. They were beheld in a new, truer light. When they were checked out during the nude poker game they had to be gazed at non-sexually, like a science project, to ensure the dick remained below leg level. It was a strict defiance of nature and a painful one too, like watching an entire porno movie without whacking off.

But the situation at hand wasn't like that at all. It seemed to concur with natural law, or to at least whatever laws do or don't take place in the sleepwalking condition of 5:00 a.m. Suspended in an unfamiliar place, in an addled state of mind, the rules and expectations of the waking world didn't necessarily apply. Anyway, by the time Darrell regained consciousness, all drunken high jinks of the mad night before would exist only as some forgotten dream.

Except Darrell was awake, watching the whole thing, Liz told me later. How could he have lain there, without objection? He should have clocked me with an armchair as I was sucking her tit, causing a nipplectomy. Or kicked the back of my head when we were French kissing, so we were spitting teeth. I swear I wouldn't have protested any and all such responses from the little guy. At least for Chissakes scream what whores and louses we were and tear off in the car, with tires screeching punctuations. Face it—it's a bit odd watching a scene like that without *some* form of protest. Was he planning to intercede just before her third orgasm? ("No woman of mine triple climaxes with another feller, wise guy!!" Kapow!) Was he taking notes, like a sociology project? ("April 3rd. 0453 hours. It has become apparent I've been botching the oral sex phase by tonguing the clit with excessive pressure. Perhaps it is this that has made her stray.") I guess only Darrell knows for sure.

Actually it's not funny. Darrell in fact, never mentioned the situation to me, so I had to endure the entire brunt of the guilt trip with no mitigating factors. He was incapable of being the asshole I wouldn't have *minded* fucking over. Liz wasn't overly guilt ridden or sympathetic. She from the start was stringing old Darrell along so she could hang with the rest of us. And the sad truth is Darrell surely knew it too, and simply lived with it. The poor, honest soul has accepted this way of life from day one. So it's up to the non-Darrells, people like me who already view the cluster of humanity as cynically as anyone, to protect these sweet souls trudging with extra weight of the cold world by warding off come-ons from chicks like Liz or so-and-so's wife or girl, upholding one ethical standard that actually has some merit. In my eyes, only one moral prescription survives inexactitude: whatever you do that causes another person pain is immoral. And despite the spear AOP tosses through many a traditional value, one constant is that no one gets hurt. I can't recall another time the hedonism of AOP was manifested at the expense of another. I fucked over a friend, and thus myself. One can't do the first without the latter. With all the sweet pickings available, I chose the poison apple. Such a lack of self-restraint causes civilizations to tumble down on deserving souls.

The following Christmas eve, everyone evacuated Fort Collins except for Darrell and me, so we had dinner together. He and Liz had long since split. I gave him about five of my CDs for presents, awkwardly trying to make the still-unspoken thing right. I probably would have worked to pay part of the fucker's tuition had he asked. Strangely, he never showed an ounce of malice towards me. It was maddening. The bastard was some kind of martyr or something. So I whipped up a big, delicious pot of spaghetti, the best I'd ever made, and served up a pre-Christmas feast with a lot of beer and some good, loud tunes to scarf by. It was outstanding. Hell, at that point, what else could one do??

28

Most students choose to involve themselves with activities signifying college life. And none of these activities imparts more excitement than college football. Like a religion, most AOPers would awake inordinately early on fall Saturdays and caravan to the game. Unfortunately, we'd seldom actually venture inside the stadium, because the tailgate parties in the parking lot were near impossible to leave. The things ran before, during and after the games. In the evening we'd be out clubbing, telling some chicks we spent all day at the football game. "Really? Who won?" they'd inquire. We hadn't a goddamned clue.

Except for one game, when two girls picked up Wilt and me while tailgating, then dragged us in to attend the second half. Sitting in the stands, someone mentioned how exciting it would be to make out on the green pasture at the 50-yard line.

"We'll get trampled!" Wilt blurted.

"I mean after the game." So afterward we did so, and it was intensely romantic, or at least until it clicked we were rolling around in the sweat and blood of a bunch of 300-pound linemen.

But it was cool seeing part of a game for a change. For first time game goers unsure how to behave at these things, don't panic—fitting in is easy, if that's your bag. It's not even necessary to remove your eyes from your honey or your beer. It's like this: if the crowd cheers madly, that's when you release some whoops and hollers of your own. For a brief period you can howl like a rabid mutt in front of 50,000 strangers and not get carted away. Take full advantage of it. If the crowd majority stands and cheers, do likewise and thrust your fist over the head for impact. If a collective groan obviously disagrees with the ref's call, simply yell "Bullshit!" and thrust the arm forward, with the index finger extended accusingly. Don't gouge the lady in front of you. Armed with this basic information, it's not even obligatory to pay mind to the game at all.

Football games and other like sports are clever forums tailor-made for downing truckloads of beer. People such as AOPers who normally tailgate in the parking lot for five hours straight are labeled wretched drunks by the general public, a point difficult to debate. Yet someone drinking similar beer portions while cheering on the home team is considered a devoted sports fan. Think about it: Why be a wretched drunk when you can be a devoted sports fan?

The cheerleaders are the real show. One wonders how these strange anachronisms survived the cynical waters of the past 30 years, but ultimately becomes glad they did. You just can't help but appreciate the fine simplicities they impart with their broad, toothy smiles. I've spent entire games mesmerized by these bubbly adults skipping and leaping about on the sidelines. They do it straight facedly, with no sense of irony, somehow keeping their self-respect fully intact. As a spectator, it's an experience bound by equal parts love, lust, empathy, envy and horror. It's best to take the situation at face value, without contemplation.

One inevitable sight at football games is large contingents of Greeks. Greek football fans are easily identified by their tee shirts—invariably the fronts are stamped with large letters spelling hard-to-pronounce words. Two guys with like letters on their tees occupy the same Greek organization, called a *fraternity*. The female equivalent of the fraternity is the *sorority*. Here are some descriptive words I might use for fraternity members: "courteous," "conservative," "goal-oriented," "sometimes kinda wild" and "business-minded." Those in different walks of life might add "conscientious" and "dopey." But never "tragedy." For starters, "tragedy" isn't even an adjective. On the other hand, Tyce's decision to join a frat after his first semester at CSU could rightly be described as a tragedy. A Greek tragedy, in the truest sense. It was a strange, sad turn for a fellow who otherwise had his head on straight.

Tyce, Don and I were hitching back from a football game (having lost our ride) one Saturday afternoon, when the bomb went off—"By the way fellahs, I'm thinking about joining the ATOs next semester." He said it off-handedly, like an announcement to buy a loaf of bread or something. It was an awkward, alien statement that didn't fit with the immediate surroundings—square words being forced out of a round hole that was his mouth. They emitted a painful resonance. I choked a bit on a beer nut; even Don's cool demeanor became frazzled for a half second. He didn't respond with an actual word, he just released a soft groan before composing himself. Tyce trotted on like a kid heading home from a ball game, not missing a stride. The guy was ice. It was the type of nonchalance seen in Bogart movies. My and Don's minds reeled backwardly in search of an explanation, to the events of the morning, of recent months. Did Tyce hear the Greeks chortle an especially appealing fight song at the game that rendered them suddenly irresistible? Did he procure a raw need to master their secret handshakes? We needed answers; Tyce offered few clues. Something had stricken the poor boy's condition, and like with a cancer victim, we could only look on sympathetically.

Thinking back, his announcement wasn't that farfetched. Tyce always carried armfuls of contradictory elements, and never seemed the least bit strained by the load. The only crystal clear thing about

Tyce was that at this life stage, casual sex, music and partying were the only things he took seriously. Everything else was highly varied means to these fundamental ends. And he'd even occasionally renege on the Big Three principles, when he'd find himself mired in a one or two-month-long relationship. These would of course fizzle when the chick would finally catch him cheating. But strangely, his philandering was accomplished so non-maliciously, his girlfriends would never get too angry about it. Rather than considering it a betrayal, they viewed it as a need to gratify a primordial appetite that they, try as they might, were unable able to do alone. So, rather than bitterness, a kind of maternal disappointment resulted.

Tyce's decision to join a frat too caused more disappointment than anger from his friends. It's just that a move towards unoriginality, plainness and convention seemed so unbefitting for the guy. But although his enlistment was initially depressing, the story actually has an upbeat ending. Because Tyce became the worst frat boy maybe ever, just being himself.

The great honest thing about Tyce was he was severely unschooled in the frat-specializing practice of preconceived typecastings and judgmental opinings. His mindset was somehow disengaged from the elements that separate humanity. He truly labeled nothing (unlike your pigheaded author), and expected no labels to be assigned to him. He could hang with a poetry-reading freak one moment and an uptight, conservative Greek kid the next, fully oblivious to all social ramifications. No one's had the heart to break it to him that's not the way the fucked-up world operates. Tyce conformed not a whit to frat land, remaining true to his disjointed demeanor and many-jointed lifestyle. He resisted all moderating influences and conversions of personality; if anything, the group and its time-honored methods somehow adapted to *him*.

Getting Tyce to pledge ATO was analogous to a pro team signing the Heisman trophy winner. Tyce was infinitely better looking and more charismatic than his "brothers," and would be an instant force. He would elevate the group's credibility as a whole, in turn increasing the value of individual members. His membership would appeal to potential recruits, ensuring quality future pledges. His cool manner and charm towards women would neutralize some of the geeky elements of the organization. His enlistment was good for the fraternity business, plain and simple.

Shamefully, Tyce was a jet-black sheep, and dangerously so. His clean-cut look and old-west ways sinisterly closed the subversive sale of messing with authority, before-lunch partying and multi-partner sex. He'd get these clean-cut frat types stoned beyond recognition and present them with a full-blast The Doors' American Prayer—an *out-there* poetry album—messily toying with their well-polished value system. So his tenure cast a rude spin on the previously understood concepts of convention and normality in the fraternity arena.

And "normal" is precisely what ATOs and other Greeks organizations generally seek. For these organizations espouse a classic middle-of-the-road philosophy. Most members are non descript sorts who make a good fit, rather than offer unique contributions. Fraternities are made up of everyday sorts; most study business. Contacts m' boy. They happily embrace the horrid sectionalism last seen in high school—the cliqueishness the rest of the college population is relieved to escape. So they naturally despise cool sorts who aren't Greek— they find their non-enlistment a personal affront. Fratheads are majority-opinion types who evade controversy, anything too extreme. Adapting to the already-drafted dictums of the organization is the key. Generally, a no-risk approach to life is maintained. This doesn't imply that fratheads are all straight-laced goody goody sorts; many are hard drinkers and drugsters alike. In fact lots of these folks assume they're the wildest pack of ruling crazies around. They're deluded, however, because directions have been pre-determined and choices pre-made. The Art, my friend, is conspicuously lacking from their Partying.

The territoriality Greeks employ is as patriotic as apple pie. In fact it's intrinsic to all group chemistry. Part of the bonding process of The Group is the denigration of those apart from it. This occurs on micro levels—people solidifying friendships by slamming a third party, and on a macro level, with the solidarity of nationalism or patriotism cemented by rejection of the outsider. It's an age-old bonding process. But Tyce wasn't burdened by such social intricacies; they only interfered with his carefree existence. Tyce was oblivious to his Greek failings, but somehow his type was unhealthy for this many-century-old organization steeped in tradition. And his overwhelming charm and influence made his participation almost seditious. A few more recruits like Tyce planted about, and the entire Greek system might have very well flushed down the toilet.

As a side note, one reassurance should be made to the parents of a student deciding to go Greek. It's a widespread belief that the members of two distinct fraternal organizations will fight to the end when their paths cross, not unlike the Crips and the Bloods, or the Jets and the Sharks. That if, for example, an Alpha Omega Omega Tri-Omega Epsilon happens to share a library elevator with a Gamma Gamma Gamma Gamma Gamma Gamma Gamma, by the time the desired floor is reached, the weaker one'll be slumped in the corner, a Bic pen lodged in his temple. This is poppycock. On the contrary, these folk as a rule respect all that is Greek and whatever is potentially Greek. Though someone may run with another Greek pack, he still has a Greek heart and Greek sensibilities. He for certain ain't no pinko *non*-Greek. It ain't the letters on the shirt that matter, it's the letters in the alphabet: alpha, beta, dufus, etc. So, straightening the matter out, it's the *non*-Greeks who should be checking their backs in elevators.

29

Midway through the spring semester I secured a part-time job, attempting to raise my standard of living from bum level to poverty level. Employment opportunities are scarce in Fort Collins, so when a janitorial job for the dorm opened up, I jumped on it. My boss's name was Wanda, and she was possibly the sweetest lady on earth— probably a born againer or something but very loving—sort of a mother-away-from-home for lots of her student employees. I'd report on Tuesdays and Thursdays, when Wanda would issue me special cleaners and scrub brushes and give me a pep talk regarding the ongoing need to combat dirt. She was damned convincing—her staff approached cleaning with an uncommon fanaticism. I was among a huge network at Westfall Hall including electricians, carpenters, plaster-repairmen, glass-smiths and fire-extinguisher specialists who all spent a good chunk of their day toiling on west 11. The administration would have done better to install a satellite maintenance office right there on the floor. In the bizarre, cyclical economy of the dorms, the shameless fuck-ups on our half of 11 ensured that food and shelter existed for a certain percentage of the Fort Collins populace.

Towards the end of the school year, Westfall sponsored an awards ceremony, in which students voted by ballot for categories like "Most likely to stumble in at 6:00 a.m.," etc. Our floor voted in unison, thus raking in most of the awards. We bought a big jug of whiskey to celebrate our inevitable victories, and after a few-shot appetizer stormed the cafeteria doors just before the dinner ceremony. We passed the bottle around like pirates, pelted other tables with food, etc. Standard college high jinks, no more, no less by our account. And prime fodder for the disapprovers who attempt to pierce your skull with a laser beam of concentration, hoping your brain turns to dust.

Unfortunately, sweet Wanda was also amid this flight of stares. Befriending pleasant, respectable people is a bittersweet experience for an AOPer, knowing odds are you'll completely repulse them somewhere down the line. They meet your sober half and decide he's the most gentlemanly, well-mannered sort around—even a possible suitor for their daughter now away at bible school. Then the other half emerges, and they dash for the hills, howling. But I honestly thought the awards ceremony was relatively restrained and orderly. And other than the mouthful of whiskey I spewed at Kile across the table while gurgling, "Drown, bastard," I thought my personal conduct was fairly pedestrian.

I reported to work that Tuesday, fresh and pumped for some serious cleaning. Wanda's face was sullen and serious. Some of the color had left it. I thought maybe her son had just kicked it or something. It was hell for her, but she finally disclosed she would have to let me go, on account of my appalling behavior at the dinner. She even mentioned in her chaste way that she was certain my wang presented itself that night, muscling its way out of the long-john getup I was wearing. I doubted that—my long-john fly seals up tight—but anything's possible. It just miffed me how someone could be so solemn while discussing such a goofy thing. Even if an early stage of her thought processes could find a cafeteria wang-on-the-loose amusing, her 45 years of training in respectability and righteousness would override such devilish impulses and produce the end-notion that the matter was grave, and one to be reckoned with. At the moment our differences were never clearer, yet I felt uniquely bonded to her and relieved she was apart from the unsettled world of whiskey dinners and publicly flopping penises.

Standing there I felt contrite, but I also found a peculiar appeal in her maternal, nun-like demeanor. I wanted to rock in her soft arms while nursing a breast or something. She was teary and forlorn, and I felt even worse that she was so worked up over a rogue-clown like myself. I kind of consoled her with a reassuring hug, which was odd considering it was *my* ass that just got canned. That Wanda was a fucking genius at firing someone, that's for sure.

30

Wanda's gesture was purely academic, as school was out in two weeks anyway. Tyce was spending his senior year in the ATO frat house. Wilt had an off-campus abode lined up; most of the others from 11 were also scattering off-campus. Cyndi was transferring to a school in Arizona, while Don was joining some hometown friends in a house in the foothills. My own future at CSU was as hazy as the past. At the time I believed mobility was the answer to everything and (still tentatively) planned to continue a westward progression to a California university in the fall. I had applied to various west-coast schools along with UC Boulder, and was awaiting responses. I was heading to Hawaii for the summer to visit my sister and two brothers. The plan was to drive to California and leave the van with a family friend. Wilt was spending the summer in New York with his dad. Tyce'd head to Denver spending the break with his parents.

On the last day in the dorms, I awoke around 9 a.m. and while heading to the can saw a familiar form in the hall. After some scrutiny, I realized it was Tyce, sans his mustache. "What happened to your car?" I asked.

"I smashed in the *left* quarter panel last night," he solemnly replied. Mine was an educated guess. Friend's of Tyce came to understand the removal of his 'stash was invariably linked to further deterioration of The Gray Ghost. His parents bought the car for him/ he was wracked with guilt/ his mom didn't like the 'stash—it didn't take a psychology major to tie elements of Tyce's behavior in a crazy knot. The act was also a ritual in self-mutilation, since he looked positively pedestrian without it. It really changed his face, his entire look dramatically.

But it was checkout day in this mad hotel, and people were frantically bustling about like beavers, packing things up and hauling them out. Don and Renny had already left. "So you coming back or what?" Tyce called over from his side of the suite to mine, as we were folding clothes. He heard I was leaving; this was the first talk of it ever. I never made it clear to anyone.

"I honestly couldn't tell you," and it was the truth. It was strange. Our communication level always respected a realm of sparse coolness; the downside was that everyday information regarding one another was often a complete mystery. So as we dutifully packed our belongings, it finally kicked in that this might be the conclusion of the short, wild ride that was our friendship. We had a 12-pack of tepid beers left from the night before, and after five minutes of petty shirt folding and sock pairing said a simultaneous "fuck it," and went for the beer. We extracted the huge couch from our suite that we borrowed from Corbett Hall in our first week and set it directly in front of the eleventh-floor elevator. We piled the warm beers on the floor and parked on the beer-stained sofa, staring forth at the double doors.

"Ding!" People appeared momentarily with footlockers, duffel bags, stacked high. They had worried, hurried looks on their faces. "Pop!" went a beer top. Few words were spoken. We mainly wanted to sit, drink and watch the elevator traffic. "Ding!" Tracy, the dorm nymphomaniac appeared with her oblivious parents. They looked upstanding. "Pop!" "Pop!" "Ding!" More parents arrived to rescue their children. We were starting to get drunk and glassy eyed and to slouch. The stop on 11 was getting to be a mighty poor advertisement for the school. "Ding!" "Hi Tyce, hey Mick," a daughter suggestively sang. We returned raspy hellos with cigarette-and-beer etched voices. Her father accusingly eyed the two bus-stop idiots. By 4:00 o'clock the place was nearly empty; we knew we had to get moving. We disposed of the couch diagonally in an elevator and slowly packed up the rest of our belongings. It was an emotional sad/happy moment. Maybe the last time I saw the unique Tyce and all of my good Midwestern neighbors dinging their way toward the rows of cars in the lot.

Yet at least at this age, there's something exhilarating about approaching and leaving a place, a town—it's got a noble air to it. Great, raw joy wrapped the moment I arrived in Fort Collins only months back—my brother and I on-the-roaded it from back east to California, a dull ride until Colorado, when I-70 becomes a self-driven roller coaster—as the overloaded van clacks up the mountain at 35 mph—and then crests the peak and barrages down at 100, hugging guard rails, a battering ram of get-outta-the-way power on a no-brake coast through Grand Junction, into Utah and finally into the campground of Zion National Park. After a two-day break it was on through the barren steam of the August desert, the rolled-window wind doing nothing to cool, just flapping flappy things in the back of the van for hours until someone cracks and reaches back to remedy it. After trucking through Vegas, Los Angeles was only hours away; I dropped off Graham under a 100 foot palm by the beach, and skidded a 3/4 U-turn towards I-80 and northern Colorado.

At 10:00 p.m. two days later I rolled into a KOA campground north of Fort Collins and walked its woodsy perimeter. The map of the sky shifted only an inch on the ride from the coast, but the new night was darker and brighter at its starry top. I crawled into the yard-wide tunnel in the van, surrounded by all my earthly possessions and of course couldn't sleep—I felt like a birthday kid with an unwrapped present on his lap.

And then tiptoeing into town the next day on strange streets—scenes that would assume a different everyday look in no time—with these funny friendly Midwesterners packed away in chimneyed houses—braced for the impending elements; folks whose great great great grandfathers took wagon trains westward through foreign lands and reached the forbidding wall of the Rockies, convincing them they've traveled far enough. And eventually these outsiders developed their own methods of speech and faith and lifestyle that in a blend became uniquely Coloradoan.

Now it's new generations roaming the aisles at Safeway, picking fruit the easy way—the big market the best place for a newcomer to view a cross-section of the populace—and I may be mistaken but gawd there's a huge crop of blond cuties here—they look like ego-less southern Californians equipped with an extra layer of cushion on the hiney for the cold winter ahead. The vision melded any conflicting emotions into just one of sheer exhilaration. It became a rare moment unattached to expectation—it seemed any which way life chose to unfurl itself would be the right way.

I did expect more mountains for Chrissakes, in fact there weren't *any*, except for some foothills in the distance. It seems I was swindled by some fast-talking college catalogue. But on first, second and third glance, it was a swell place to lay me boots for a while. The university dominated the tiny town, and forced an entire spectrum of people-types to coexist: the old-west cowboy, the tie-died Frisbee heads and everyone in-between. Anyone awed by life's extremities couldn't help but be smitten.

And now reckless, ambivalent—choosing to part with these simple store browsers with their own tried and true brand of gladness, those comfortably settled in for generations amid huge families and neighbors and childhood friends always there to lend an ear, with existences carefully balanced in careful moderation, praying to the heavens a tornado or earthquake or sudden death doesn't impose its disruption—what does the harsh, outside world outside have to offer that can't be found here? What makeup is a man, unable to appreciate these modest contentments and happinesses? Why must I root such things out like one would a robber-fugitive, with frothing horses in full stride and Indian trackers and dogs yapping in the moonlight, seeking trace footprints in this and any town?

But eight months had passed, and the road was calling. The rational reasons were that I wanted a university with a better humanities department, I wanted the coast, I wanted a hipper town like Boulder. But I mainly wanted to move on—to just keep going. Find another place identical to this nutty little college town: worthy enough to revel in thoroughly, yet smattered with the right amount of imperfections to allow leaving. In the restless, short-sweet time of now, such is the ideal place to live.

31

I wasn't accepted to the University of California system, and, typically, the Boulder application was received a day after the cut-off date. So, in mid-August I informed CSU I was coming back for another round. I flew into Los Angeles a week later, allowing the two-day drive to Colorado. I rolled into Fort Collins around 11 p.m. and headed straight to Wilt's new house situated across the street from campus. A large party of course was spilling into the neighbor's yard. Rusty, drunk and wild-eyed, was on the lawn, and rubbed his eyes in disbelief. "Holy shit, look who came back!" he bellowed. Tyce was there, Wilt's roommates Mac and Rick, Don, Matt Liston, Liz and Barb and all their friends, Mona, even Kile and Andre, and around 15 others.

   Rusty introduced me to some new faces as "the most radical motherfucker around," I guess based on the various police incidents. Unfortunately, my ill-fated sober state left me unqualified for the job. There was a pause; the group maybe wanted a speech or something, wanted me to show them a thing or two about what it takes to be "radical." I whimpered at all the attention and mumbled with downcast eyes something about needing a drink. It was anticlimactic, to say the least.

The madman was still out in the parking lot, asleep in the van. Or maybe he was gone for good—God knows I hadn't seen him for a while. I should have downed a quart of beer before I arrived.

But in no time I relaxed and was feeling plain happy, thankful I had returned. In a world of lost souls, including me own, 'twas a fine, fun group of people before me. Wilt, in his low-key way of saying "Glad you're back," kept a strict diet of Doors on the stereo. The gang was sitting 'round the round table, throwing down shots of Canadian Mist with Old Milwaukee chasers, telling summer stories. Tyce, of course, already had a girl in tow who had heard all of last year's adventures, assuming the ones of me would never attach a face. He took off, letting her get to know me over on the couch. She quizzically examined the shy, mellow figure before her. Perhaps she had the wrong fellow. She had a notion to ID me. Shouldn't I be loudly spewing inside jokes to the dudes then sticking my head out the window and screaming after spraying beer about? I should have completed the stereotype, making the moment easier for the both of us. To make matters worse, I'd for some reason developed a penchant when undrunk for speaking one decibel over or under the audible level, so when I *do* talk, it's a battle to hear me. She leaned in. "Eh?" she said. "Eh?" The music was too loud or something. It wasn't working out. She gave up on me and went to consummate her catch. This all was my pre-whiskey self, who in general is introspective, thoughtful, quiet, considerate and, of course, boring as all sin, or lack thereof.

Wilt came over and began touting the benefits of off-campus life to me, like a demented salesman. "Check it—room to myself, king-size waterbed—no need to *ever* kick or lock out your roommates. People can coexistence here without conflict." The concept had extra appeal to me, as my present domicile was the back section of the van. He showed me around. The kitchen was already trashed, one day into the lease. A stray cigarette was hanging off the Formica counter, a minute away from etching its brown, permanent 1/2" x 3" stain. Wilt I'm sure saw it, but continued on, opting not to mess with the natural progression of things. In my acute sobriety I assumed sympathy pains for the hapless landlord. Wilt continued on to the backyard. The floodlight revealed a brown, circular stain of vomit in the grass. It had carrots in it. "Watch your step, man."

·Terry Mason, a friend from Westfall, was by the garage making out with a chick named Melody. It caught Wilt's attention. "Yo Melody, this is Mick, the guy I was telling you about who wasn't supposed to come back." Her shirt was unbuttoned all the way down; the bra was unfastened in the front. She freed herself from Terry, tossed on a crooked smile, and shyly, politely, stuck out her hand. No effort was made to redo the bra, but dumb luck had it her jugs were so big, the taut, black fabric refused to release them. So the lateral halves of each breast were still covered, along with both damned nipples. I shook her hand with maybe a bit more vertical motion than was required, hoping to free things up. Just then, a deafening crash of plate glass from the living room, sending Wilt sprinting for the house. I gazed up at the strange sky, still shaking the crazy chick's hand. Yeah, the school year started just about right.

32

In the morning I pondered the scene with Tyce's girl the night before. It was like a social impotence. Maybe I was just out of practice from the summer, but times like that emphasized how great the burden of being "entertaining" was becoming. Whoever the fuck emerges after midnight on weekends sure ain't around the rest of the time. It's strictly a part-time job. People perpetually like that are another species, craving the center of attention, like a drug. The real me is the complete fuckin' opposite. I hate all that shit. And it's a problem when the Friday night bozo picks up the girl who wants a 24-hour clown. I've wakened with many a woman who expect some superhero to be next to them in the morning. It's figured maybe I'll catch a bite to eat then go out and direct traffic on College Avenue while bellowing "Roadhouse Blues" again. It can't be done, because in the morning it's clear such behavior increases the potential of either getting killed, arrested, or both. And Christ, with *that* fucked-up attitude, one *deserves* such a fate.

    I can't figure it, but after tying a good one on, the next morning I can't assemble a decent sentence for anything. The mouth was going full tilt the night before, but somehow while sleeping or screwing the syntax switch gets bumped. You try and tell the girl in the morning "I had a perfect time", and it comes out "It's a perfect time for had," and she bops you with the pillow, thinking you're insatiable. Actually, if over six words are uttered before noon it's a good sign, reversed order or not. So the first-runner-up at the comedy improv eight hours prior turns out to be a fake—he's instead this pensive, moody lug who when he *does* speak says things backwards. Weekend mornings, for me at least, are pretty humorous.

I thought that this morning incoherence was a unique characteristic, until I mentioned it to Wilt. But he admits he's got the same affliction. He faces it head-on however, and spends weekend morns calling up various aunts and nieces, all equipped with deciphering charts to determine exactly what he's saying. He's pathetic to listen to, as they volley hyper-emotional conferences during which he sobs and laughs in the same paragraph. He's like a chick two days before she goes on the rag when he's goddamned hungover. And the girl he picked up just sits at the breakfast table through all this, reading the cereal box.

Tyce doesn't seem to share this a.m. talking problem, and is a fairly confident orator hungover, hungover in conjuction with three large bong hits, stone drunk, stoned, stoned/drunk, sober and any remaining times. Yet Tyce, armed with this very versatile gift of gab, remained cool, making no overt efforts to court the attentions of others or to brag about his past-night escapades. But post-partying morns produced plenty of voyeur-types, itching for vicarious adventure. So, being a charitable soul, Tyce'd patiently saddle up somewhere until some admirers would succumb to temptation and ask him about the preceding night. Then, of course, once the ball was rolling, he'd hold court for the rest of the morning.

Wilt and I resisted providing Tyce this fodder, since we generally campaigned against spilling the beans all over the neighborhood upon getting one's dick wet. But Tyce's behavior remained true to AOP standard for this reason: since Tyce never *doesn't* get laid, and since commonplace matters aren't celebrated, any reports of such aren't really bragging. He gets laid so matter-of-factly, little amusement value can actually be tagged to the act itself. The event alone was as routine as the 6:00 o'clock news. But even Wilt and I conceded that his stories begged a listen, since Tyce nearly always had some bizarre thing happen to him while pursuing his catch. Make that always.

My theory is this: Tyce had such an austere, stern-schoolmaster upbringing, that he now, astray from the path of righteousness, had to forever devise ways of fending off the accompanying guilt. It was a full-time job for the poor lad. He developed a real Freudian or Oedipal thing with his mother, who had the immense ability to psychically dispatch herself 90 miles to Fort Collins each time her son was about to spark a doob or bang a babe. Hell, this type of invasion would cause problems for *anybody*. Any time Tyce would be enroute to scoring, his mom would somehow trip up his plans. He'd always prevail, but never in a seamless, straightforward manner. While it could be assumed these predicaments were self-induced on account of his upbringing, I further believe Tyce's mother was so powerful, she could directly yank on the guy's strings, creating additional mayhem.

While living in Westfall, Tyce's parents paid a visit; before they arrived he hid all the Playboys and Penthouses in very good hiding spots. When he stepped out for a minute, his mom magically found all the magazines and placed stickers on the covers, 1) better concealing the ladies' privates, and 2) providing solid evidence she had found them. Tyce for a moment foolishly believed he could outsmart the woman. Had she stayed a full day she might have G-rated every picture on campus. Tyce knew his mother was onto every goddamned thing he ever did or considered doing, and so whatever he did was burdened with a clunky twist or a karmic episode. He was like the escaped convict forever trying to outmaneuver the wily lawman on his trail. For Tyce, it seldom was just hit the bar, ask the chick to dance, drive her home and make it with her. It was more like pick her up at the party, head home, run out of gas, start hitchhiking, get picked up by gypsies, go to their headquarters, smoke some opium with them, watch the cops raid the joint, flee and hide in the woods with the girl, where she gives him a head job in an oak tree. *Every* goddamned weekend.

33

I quickly found an off-campus apartment that had the winning feature of a volleyball court in the front lawn and lots of excellent players in the area. Off-campus life is a welcome change from the dorms, offering the great benefit of elbowroom, and your own room. With social contacts established, upper-class students usually choose this option. Two major pitfalls of off-campus life exist however, that become evident from day one. They're food and laundry.

Acquiring food is a daily necessity up through college and apparently after graduation, or so I'm told. Prior to university life, food gathering is elementary and effortless. Upon returning from school, any kitchen cupboard is opened and there it is, stacked high and deep. It's simply removed from one of the stacks and eaten. There's so much of it, some keen decision-making is required to determine what to actually scarf. The evenings are even easier: one's mother labors for an hour combining some of these products for a meal, after which it's snuffed something's not quite right. And it's not, because many foods lose they're appeal when they're so readily available. They taste shittily. It's a situation not unlike the discriminating zoo lion that rejects his supper because he did nothing to earn it. The big lazy cat knows anyway that he'll get tossed the next meal soon enough.

When one is living off campus in college, food makes an enormous leap to luxury status. This upgrade causes one's palate to widen tremendously. In a matter of a few months, anything previously on the reject list becomes scrumptious. Fish, radishes, all that shit are eaten with a mild fervor. Canine-like qualities even develop in certain students—two-day-old crusts of someone else's pizza are considered a suitable lunch. It's not a loss of self-respect, but just the driving force of hunger, which occurs from having no bucks.

Food is somewhat of a necessary evil. It's necessary, 'cause without it you get cranky and die, and it's evil 'cause it cuts into your partying money. Any AOPer with just four bucks on a Saturday afternoon surely ain't gonna blow the wad on something as inconsequential as dinner. Now's the time to get creative. Just remember, college is a lesson in survival, faith and courage. And only the hearty survive in such a place. It's getting 15 bucks to last two weeks. It's believing the trusty heap that's been on empty for two months will hang on for one more trip, on will alone. It's standing when the others are falling, and forever facing and fighting the injustice others are content to live with. It's upsetting the balance when it needs to be upset and accepting the harsh consequences, knowing your efforts will benefit future generations.

- Dining and Dashing

Students strictly opposed to dining and dashing make abrupt philosophical flip-flops when they haven't eaten for months. The great risk in d-and-d-ing is a cop saddling up to the booth behind you mid-meal, although a friend and I somehow got busted once by an ever-alert server. Another pitfall: once you've struck every all-night diner in town, resources shut down, since AOP conservatively recommends no more than one hit per semester per restaurant. Student servers don't stick around long in these places, and inserting a couple months between visits usually ensures the waitress you split on will be long gone. Old-hag servers, however, can stay for years, so stick to sections serviced by a student. It's also suggested to stay clear of IHOPs. Cops live in these joints. And finally, remember that a well-tipped waitress who was stiffed for the check is less likely to chuck her heels and give chase in her stockings for two miles, knocking the shit out of you and your three friends.

- Dumpster Diving

This sounds a lot worse than it is. Fast food joints like McDonald's toss out perfectly good wrapped burgers at the end of the night, ready for your microwave. Wilt and I corrected this wasteful behavior at one McDonald's dumpster with such regularity that its rearranged contents became obvious to the management. One late night we searched for half an hour; there were no quarter pounders, no Big Macs, not even a fuckin' fish fillet to be found. Finally, we discovered one wrapped burger bun that had a red piece of yarn planted inside. "We've been had!" we cried, as we dropped to our knees, arms outstretched to the heavens. Eventually we composed ourselves, and countered with a mighty leak on the backdoor of the building.

- Safeway Write-offs

Safeway has always had a buy-one-get-one-free policy, except the free merchandise has to be stashed in the coat without its employees seeing you. It's a little game the corporation thought up, and it can be fun and challenging to play. Gamblers enjoy this type of fun; how it works is that you get to keep all the stuff unless you're caught hiding it. If you're caught hiding it, you give it back to Safeway and a town official officially records it and charges you a fee. They call it a *fine* but it's far from fine, in fact it sucks. If you're caught doing it again you then pay a bigger fee, and if it happens still again sometimes you get sent to a locked room for a few months to allow you to work on your faulty strategy, or to decide the game is no fun anymore.

- Soup Kitchens

For the truly hard up. Even *I've* never been this desperate, but I know a few students who have. Or maybe they just went for the stimulating conversation. If you go, don't wash for a week and wear a ripped shirt that says "Molly Hatchet—The World Tour." You won't raise an eyebrow.

- Cooking

This is kind of a last resort. Cooking yourself is a drag 'cause number one it's actually quite difficult learning how to cook decently. Also, pre-college existence dictated the plates and utensils were washed *after* you ate; in college these things are fished out of a foot of slime-water plugged up in the sink and then washed *before* you eat. This makes dining at home a huge chore and barely worth it. I find although I'm constantly broke, I eat out nearly always. I just make sure that at the beginning of the year I file through the orientation room about 60 times to get a whole backpack full of coupon books. With these things, you can always chomp for two or three bucks a meal. Eating in college is incidental—something to get out of the way, to get on to other things. It only takes on a desperate importance after you've been partying all night, at 4 a.m. But if money is *really* tight, one has little choice but to make a huge pot of spaghetti to live on for a week, whereas your roommate, pissed that you tied up the only pot, will pour it into 15 separate bowls strewn about the fridge. Like I said, it's seldom worth the hassle.

But at least food when found has a built-in reward system. Doing laundry, on the other hand, has nearly no redeeming qualities. The clean socks get appreciated for a day, then immediately revert to being the albatross around the neck. This very great burden exists in the dorm as well as the off-campus dwelling, but the dorm has a laundry room, so the logistics of getting the clothes to and from the machines aren't as complicated. Off-campus life tosses a distant Laundromat into the formula, rendering it a chore usually dodged until a near-emergent situation is faced, that of having to wear the V-neck granny sent you for Christmas.

Not doing laundry is part of the college experience. I mean, over time the clothes get washed, but not before a host of energies have been employed to avoid the chore. Newfound independence partially explains the phenomenon—finally having the free will to not do something without being nagged about it. But the psychological ramifications of laundry avoidance run deeper than those attached to general procrastination. Failure to address one's laundry situation creates a domino effect. So suddenly, the simple act of blowing the wash off extends to all other non-fun events, in exponential fashion. And a huge, inextinguishable wildfire is the end result.

To clarify: Say you've gotta do wash, need to write a paper, should respond to a couple letters and need to fix the flat on your bike. For weeks. And since its onset, hundreds of other things have joined the list, including studying for upcoming finals. See, the likelihood of you doing anything constructive during this period is actually around 3/4 less than it was a couple weeks ago. Two weeks ago nothing also got accomplished, but there was a moderate chance that it would. Now just *thinking* about the list gives you a fucking headache. The point is reached when scratching one or two things off the scroll is like using a spoon to level a mountain. It becomes almost mandatory to quickly free your mind of the entire situation by getting a sixer and motoring to the lake.

But this lengthy, ever-present list of put-off items possessed by the college student invariably revolves around the item always topping it: doing the stinking wash. It's the most perseverant, pain-in-the-ass chore on God's green earth. It influences one's entire existence. Its need is not subtle; i.e. it can't be tossed in the background and forgotten for weeks at a time like homework. Reminders grace the entire apartment—the lack of undies, the checkered pair of shorts hanging solitarily over two six-foot heaps of clothes, the ever-present odor of dirty socks—it's insufferable.

Regarding laundry, certain methods can assist the process of not doing it. I employ a two-pile laundry system, one for clothes that are questionable and one for clothes that absolutely cannot be warn again before cleaning. After a wash is initially done, the first "dirty" pile formed is the questionable pile. After three weeks or so, the pile gains appeal, when the clean garments hanging over it become unsightly. A desirable item is fished out, put through a sniff and wrinkle test, and, if it passes, is worn. If it fails it's tossed into a neighboring pile, called the putrid pile. Any clothes extracted from the questionable pile always find the putrid pile after an additional wearing, no questions asked. When the questionable pile is gone, you either gotta buy more clothes or submit to doing wash.

Various living factors determine what makes a once-worn garment questionable or off limits. Loose button-down shirts don't reek of BO as quickly as tighter ones. Tank tops, devoid of pits, are more reusable than Tees. Weather permitting, I cruise during the day in rubber Hawaiian slippers, limiting the sock output. If possible, I maintain a clear-drink policy in bars or at parties, such as gin or vodka tonics, so the shirt inevitably sloshed on is no worse for wear. Red wine drinkers and strawberry margarita lovers I find to be puzzling breeds.

Newer shirts don't BO as quickly as older shirts. I have no idea why. Shoewise, it's a fact (for right-handers) that left shoes long outlast right shoes since the latter receives regular drink dousings at parties. Because of this, I've made regular attempts at purchasing shoes separately, with no luck and many a dirty look. Keep in mind when buying shoes that leather stands the disintegrating effects of alcohol better than suede. A tip: if your right suede shoe is apparently ruined by your right-handed drink, toss the *pair* of shoes in the washer, then dry on "industrial." The suede ones evolve into leather ones, essentially providing a spanking new style of footwear.

Variations on anti-laundry systems exist, some of dubious practice. An oddball friend rejects the two-stack theory out of laziness, and desperately fishes for underwear in one huge, smelly stack, turning them inside out this time around. Any undies encountered with opposing skid marks, that is to say a *dual* skid, he deems off limits. I hate to judge, but this is abominable. Now when one takes a dump and offhandedly notices a skid on the skivvies, it's at first a bit unnerving. The reason he or she can yank up the briefs and continue on rests on the justification that since the asshole assumes a normal state of stinky foulness, the skid, only millimeters away, somehow meshes with that world. A skid facing outward, however, crosses lines, causing disorder and confusion. It's alarming, and socially repulsive. In fact it's akin to riding on a packed bus and farting in a seated person's face, instead of politely revolving the ass before ripping loose. I don't think that's stretching it, either.

34

The varied manifestations of the AOP personality became clear over time. Wilt, Tyce and I happened to share the common experience of having a sober nature the complete opposite of the partying one. It was a Grand Canyon-like gulf. Tyce, however, maintained the slightest spread; he was neither as reticent as Wilt and me while sober nor as rowdy while drunk. Wilt and I had to traverse great miles of serpentining gray matter to reach the desired target—a cruel, often exhausting ride. It became necessary to design a method to reliably reach our destination without falling off the edge of the road. For AOP has no tolerance for people unaware of their capacities and capabilities. What we're talking about here is "buzzwork."

Buzzwork is more technique than art. The principle goal in buzzwork is attaining the crispness, the clarity of the buzz. "Buzz Crispness," or BC, is the state in which you're feeling amped and joyously confident and infallible at a club. It's the difference between tipsily swaying in the shadows of the bar, immersed in the insecurity and doubt of a sober person, and self-assuredly taking control of the place. Drinking haphazardly, paying no heed to buzzwork, often produces a syndrome known as "The Drunken Feeling," or TDF. TDF, the converse of BC, is a stumbling, tired, slurred-worded waste-of-a-night that's common to alchies. It's a fate to be avoided at all costs by the AOPer. Yet the inexperienced partier can fall victim to such a syndrome without proper precautions.

Paying mind to a few AOP ABCs nearly guarantees BC over TDF. The most common scenario resulting in TDF is when a student drinks during say a Saturday football game, then expects the usual buzz that night at the bars. It won't happen. The problem is that the day's "peak pocket" was spent. A peak pocket is the period where one's seratonin activity (uniquely synthesized with the tequila) is at its most heightened level. It's an immensely energetic feeling of well being. Unfortunately, only one peak pocket exists per person per day, and once it's spent, most attempts to revive it only lead to TDF. Daytime partiers seeking an *additional* peak pocket must take an evening nap (even just a 20 minute one works), preferably right after dinner. This cheats the body into thinking it's another day, and another peak pocket is made available.

Optimal buzz clarity is achieved approximately one-and-a-half hours after a good-sized meal. It's best to avoid alcohol directly before, during or after eating. If downed immediately following a meal it takes twice as much alcohol to do the job, and the buzz is often dull, disappointing, and headed for late-night TDF. Shots with beer chasers are the preferred method of ingestion, with tequila edging out scotch for buzz quality. Clear alcohol offers a diminished hangover, but the buzz is slightly compromised.

Before the action gets underway, the shots are ingested. A common mistake is hitting the party sober, intending to tie one on at the scene. Bringing the moody, sober personality anywhere near a party or club can result in difficulty getting it to leave, even when you're buzzed. The tag-along little shit can easily screw up an entire night. So the shots are done beforehand in the living room, with The Doors blasting at explosive volumes. They're ideally administered on a half-full stomach at five-minute intervals, for a good 45 minutes. A good indicator: when four people are present, a 1.75 liter bottle should be half drained before taking off for the shindig. During the course of the night, only a maintenance buzz should be necessary, with beer sufficing. If maintenance includes shots, sticking to the same type of liquor is desirable.

This is the only method sanctioned by AOP. It's cost effective for the budget-conscious student. It achieves premium buzz clarity, and minimizes possibilities of The Drunken Feeling. It ensures the sober, uptight ass-wipe is cordoned away from the scene. And hangovers are minimized, with limited mixings of liquors.

A word about hangovers: Hangovers are only the body's reaction to change, a rejection of a foreign substance. The AOPer's job is to make this foreigner a citizen—to naturalize it. Regular college partying ensures minimal hangovers. Ever wonder why hangovers, specifically headaches, never occur on a second or third consecutive morning following drinking? It's because at that point the foreigner is like an old pal—all cultural differences are ironed out. Drinking sporadically is an ungratifying sport, because the next day is invariably ruined. And non-AOP partiers mistakenly blame the alcohol, when in fact the lack thereof is the culprit.

35

Drugs. Jesus Christ, these days they're akin to child molesting in terms of public popularity. Mainstream society has ingeniously reemerged the pre-1960s belief that any usage denotes imbalance and/or dependence. Sports figures caught with a joint are forced to attend rehab programs to remedy the "addiction." A growing number of businesses have jumped on the intolerance bandwagon, administering drug tests to weed out all scum who might have smoked reefer three weeks ago while listening to music. The creative mind, however, will always seek methods to enhance creativity—different angles from which to view the world. It's a trait as certain and inviolate as any law on the books.

Now it's obvious hyper-addictive sorts have no business messing with drugs (alcohol included). Instead of being enhanced by the experience, these souls are ambushed, and their personalities metamorphize defectively, terribly. It's simple with these folks—they undergo a number of fucked-up, joyless, wasted experiences, reach a low point and then either adopt sobriety or accept life as a slave. Most who choose the latter are imbalanced sorts to begin with, who only continue their self-abuse to appease the pain of general existence. For them, getting high is no relation to fun; it's just a barrier from the equally wretched but more-aware world of sobriety. But instead of accurately planting the onus on these folks' genetic predisposition, basic weaknesses or their general inability to cope, it's much handier to blame the souls' demise on the evil drugs. The benefits are twofold: mass homogenization is encouraged by demonizing alternate consciousnesses; plus the poor bastard is allowed a refreshing escape from responsibility.

So drugs, the scourge of civilized society, are deposited in one pile for easy dismissal. It makes the job of the lawmakers and do-gooders who battle them an easy one. For these simpletons, a transcendent peyote experience is indistinct from the state of the twitching, itching, street-corner crack addict. It's impossible for these automatons accept that functional, intelligent people can occasionally get high causing no harm to themselves or to others.

Fortunately, in college one develops the education and knowledge to penetrate their line of bullshit. Alcohol and drugs in college are personal choices, like majors and minors. The only drug that gets me reliably social, and thus able to attain AOP standard, is alcohol. It's a college panacea, marred only by the occasional hangover. I can't imagine picking up a woman without *some* percentage of alcohol doing laps in the bloodstream. But the healthy, curious student will usually dabble in whatever drugs he can get his hands on for a brief time, then will outgrow them. I've personally fazed out regular usage of pot, but man at times I miss those days during my freshman year sitting in a mad circle bonging our brains out, talking so intensely and especially laughing so completely, so full-bodiedly, that nothing in the large, sad world could ever conspire to stifle it. I wonder this: With each passing year, are laughs as these atrited in some cruel mathematical formula?

Despite its commonness, pot is a rather complex drug. It's remarkable in the early stages of the experience, invoking great philosophical perspectives and the aforementioned belly laughs. Unfortunately, its revelatory aspect wanes with usage, and a good amount of apathy and laziness often supplant it. The drug also encourages a subtle retreat occurs from any people or peer groups choosing to weather life non-stoned. Pot causes great extroversion around those of a like mindset, but the reverse among everyone else. Thus, it's loads of fun for folks choosing not to venture outside their groups. So over time, these sorts lapse into the same facile cliquishness they surely work overtime to denounce. Pot usage generally wanes as the college years progress, spurred by the unsettled, tottery state of not getting laid for many moons. The self-induced stoned orgasm, which is a normal orgasm times 600, is spoiling, and the coital orgasm becomes an afterthought. All is well until a "post auto-jism depression syndrome" intrudes on the solo act, which is actually enhanced by the pot. It's the body telling you to wise up and spread your seed, and not just fire it in some anonymous napkin and drown it down the toilet. It's some perpetuation of the species instinct kicking in, I believe. Of course, pot is great for two-person sex also, but only with someone you're comfortable with. The thought of actually picking up a woman while stoned is nerve-wracking, for me at least. I'd be shaking like a madman.

Coke is exhilarating the first time you do it, and goes downhill from there. One eventually realizes it's ideal for those attracted to manic-depressive states. Crank or speed is a mellower, longer-lasting coke, without the mood swings. But it stays in your system for days, creating a tense, unnatural state, always reminding you of the indulgence. Anyone interested in developing a paranoiac hatred of the world should indulge regularly. It's also the only drug that makes you horny as sin and at times virtually unable to achieve a hard-on. One can masturbate for hours to no avail, an experience that's as fascinating as it is maddening. A half-mast orgasm eventually comes only after a peak reverie of the most lewd, teen-lesbian fantasy conceivable. Opiates like heroin and opium are too addictive to mess with. Designer drugs like Ecstasy at times live up to their name, with most being variants of others. Hallucinogens are virtually mandatory on rare occasion in college to deliver perspective and large pallets of truth, but should be used carefully and sparingly.

Lots of books have been written trying to describe the indescribable—that is, the mushroom (or peyote/mescaline/acid) trip. My attempt will be equally futile. But here's a try, starting with a lame-ass analogy: The construct of life for some can be thought of as a favorite coat discovered in one's prime. Hanging on the rack in the store, the coat's color and flashy style begged for attention. Its cut and fit were superb; it was to be a magnet for the ladies. The coat was taken home, and, as predicted, enhanced all occasions requiring smartness and dapperness. As the years moseyed by, the coat's original punch waned, but it took on a practical function. It provided warmth and protection from the harsh elements of the world. It assumed the role of security blanket, a bit of predictability in a sometimes-crazy existence. And in time the thing got worn obsessively, unconsciously, to the point where any other choice of attire was inconceivable. It was slept in even. And it reeked of moth piss.

Enter the hallucinogenic. In violent assault, the drug rips off the coat and puts a match to it. It strips the soul as naked as birth, and demands the mind take a microscope to every action and occurrence, regardless of how seemingly trivial. Nothing just slips on by unnoticed. It's the nosiest drug around. Even squeezing out an offhanded dump becomes an extraordinary phenomenon.

It's astounding how many icons come crashing down. Everything's got holes in it. Societal life gets reappraised as petty and meaningless—ants in a colony. Yet oddly, the discovery is elating, as if the puzzle to existence is finally solved. "The world shall from here spin with new-found knowledge and truth."

When interacting with others, any former glossings-over become as apparent as a red banner. The drug offers no mercy. For example, if your neighbor is: 1) a decent partier, 2) an excellent joke teller, 3) an okay volleyball player and 4) a phony idiot, to the tripper he will appear only as the phony idiot. The other attributes don't register; they may just as well belong to someone else. In this regard, the drug is diametrically opposed to alcohol. Alcohol makes the neighbor more likeable. 'Shrooms find him increasingly revolting.

Quite obviously, the drug can summon disaster in the wrong hands. For a good chunk of the world, the day-to-day goings on create a rather intentional diversion to the cold, hard truths of the world. Any intimations that one's friends are shallow imbeciles and his or her own life is a sham aren't exactly redeeming. In fact, if someone suspects he and his friends are indeed shallow imbeciles, and isn't requiring of concrete proof, it's probably a better bet to just split a case of beer.

Luckily, a respite from all the heaviness occurs. For at some point, some extraordinary phenomenon conjures possibly the greatest laugh-force the human body is capable of. It's even more intense than pot-induced laughter. It's laughter so fully uncontrollable and complete, it takes on a life of its own. They are great, huge, belly-bottom laughs originating from the deepest spot of the gut and rolling upwards in waves, knotting stomach muscles, rippling in currents past the twitching larynx, past the mouth, and spilling into the room.

It takes more than relative genuineness, depth of soul and the desire to learn for a satisfactory hallucinogenic experience. Sober-minded sorts requiring absolute control of their facilities and surroundings have an excellent chance of "freaking," so to speak. All visions and lessons come abstractly, obliquely, and are unveiled in the throes of an addled, electric state of being. One hundred volts surging through the body for eight straight hours. Got too high on pot or too drunk? Hit the sack and sleep it off. Did too many 'shrooms? You're doomed to endure each dissected moment, and for a short eternity. The road to nirvana is a tortuous and sometimes torturous one, to no surprise.

Incidentally, any benefits of hallucinogens are usually received in low doses. In high, regular doses, not only is little sense made of anything, but from a certain point on a portion of the mind becomes overdone, like a tough piece of steak. If you could slip a fork prong somewhere around the temple area, the brain matter wouldn't feel spongy and pliable, as it should. It would provide a good deal of resistance, like an unripe mango. In this medium, brain cells don't transmit information efficiently. So when it's time to give the Sears credit lady your phone number of five years, the thing completely eludes you.

36

Actually, I can best illustrate one mushroom experience by means of two Dalmatians. Tyce and I were 'shrooming at a party, which is usually a lousy idea for me, since if it's possible to actually say *less* than nothing at all, that's my approximate communication level. Luckily, however, confidences were running high, unlike like the horrific feeling of being *sober* at a bash, appreciating what a dull, nervous fool you really are. This instead was introversion with security and knowledge. The mouth was fully unable to form words, but it was all some master plan of the brain. I mean, why add to the chaos at hand? The party became an entertaining spectator sport. All the nutty power plays and pecking orders became ever evident, and made for some fascinating viewing. A dramatic, crazed, funny-sad theater of life was playing right before us, and we had front row seats.

    Despite not participating in the social game, Tyce and I began to feel like deities. We may have been deluded, but we developed strong inclinations that we were shepherds and the party was our flock. The people before us were to be nobly and noiselessly tended late into the night, and kept from straying beyond the living room, kitchen or bathroom. A major task was at hand.

We immediately appointed assistants, two Dalmatians, who were clearly operating on similar levels. They were happy to help, as they seemed to have no other plans for the evening. We could easily relate to our co-workers. No inhibitions or self-consciousnesses seemed to exist for these fellows either. But they employed a more lax standard. They could lick their balls in broad view, because the public bestows no mores saying they shouldn't. Plus, they were lots more flexible than at least I am.

One of the dogs took a break and strolled into the living room, then spontaneously rubbed his itchy ass across the whole carpet, propelling himself forward with his front legs like crutches. Following the event, the dog indicated no embarrassment or remorse. His ass itched and he remedied it with directness and economy. Now it don't itch. What a wonderful life! And all this without drugs or alcohol. Tyce and I were convinced the lucky bitches were at that point showing off a bit. If *we* tried something like that, someone'd call the cops, and they knew it. The dogs had also easily figured out we were 'shrooming, with their heightened powers of sensory perception. Each mannerism, every *movement* for that matter was generated for our benefit. They sat with their hind legs wrapped up like spaghetti, then uncoiled them in slow motion. Their back legs bent the wrong way at the knee. They stalked us throughout the night like wild game then whimsically spared our lives. They were damned cagey about everything too, pretending we didn't exist for a minute, then flashing knowing glances. The people at the party thought we were just playing with the dogs.

The spots were exceptional. Somewhere beneath the hair and under the skin, somehow laid a geometrically perfect round patch of black fur follicles in a sea of white ones. And this occurred all over the place, for evolutionary reasons which made no sense at all.

I came up with a personal aphorism that night, which surely arose from our communion with the dogs. "All our worries stem from comparing ourselves with others." And I must humbly admit a truer thing was never conjured. We think with rationalized effort we can free ourselves from the impressions of nobodies we don't give a half-shit about, but it's strangely impossible. If we could, no relative dissatisfactions could plague us. AOPers are generally worry-free because they drink a lot of beer, offsetting the process. But what about when the tap runs dry? What then??

Late in the night, thoughts of the unfair world of ever-increasing responsibility impinging on guileless college students became rampant. Why not create a life as our spotted friends? We examined the possibilities. Simply use charm and appeal to ensure good meals and a place to sleep, then immerse one's self in the more important roles of playing and humping. Then still another revelation: with minor nasal adjustments, that *was* us, at least temporarily. Foolish mutts, barking at moons. No wonder we four bonded so quickly. The drug was merciless, like a kid asking too many fuckin' questions when you're trying to read the paper, and it became tiresome. Some truths are better not dwelled upon. I mean, how *will* we survive beyond the romping pastures of campus, for gawds sake??

37

Sunday, 6:00 a.m. Well into my third year in college. I'd just faced an ejection from the apartment of a girl I met the night before at a party, as her roommate was returning that morning from mom and dad's. I was hoofing it home. Tanya had the ideal weekend—she was able to address the urgings of her sex drive while keeping her reputation intact with her roommie. She was from the old school of getting laid; the new school proudly parades their hungover trophy in front of roommates, friends, parents or anyone else available in the neighborhood. Despite this chick's double-life, she was quite unambiguous about her needs the night before, and set down her philosophy on sex not long into some heavy making-out on her couch. Single women don't need sex for long periods of time, says she, and are easily able to go without for two or three straight months. It's just not a pressing issue during that period. But *after* then it's subtly sought, and once taken care of they're good to go for another quarter year. It was kind of a sterile confession, like an order for a short-term vaccine or something. We had a blast, but just before waking, I experienced a nightmare, the latest of a recurring variety that seemed to lambaste all Dionysian impulses of late. It was the kind of dream that jolts electricity in your body at 5 a.m., ending all hopes of further slumbering.

What messenger, this deliverer of remorse, of misgiving? 'Tis no part of me. And is surely no welcomed stranger. Yet he again jimmied the lock to the Church of Fulfilled Pleasure and Pointed Detachment From Responsibility, and was now preaching his stoic reproofs to all trying hard not to listen. And the fucker messed up a perfectly good conclusion to a fine rollick in the hay. It was as though daybreak herself was presiding as judge and jury over the folly of the night, of all nights, demanding repentances and atonements for all transgressions. The half-sun became a watchful, scornful eye. All ghosts had converged on a poor soul on an innocent trudge home. It was the last scene of a foolish morality play, in which the antagonist faces his bleak, deserving fate. Apart from the hiding places the great night affords, I was improbably assailed by the sweet angel of light.

Who used to be an inspiration. But now it's that one whacked-out gene inside of me who would enjoy a gentle romp in her Eden, but would never resist a swap for the revved up, smash-fest of emotion fed late night in raw form—instant delivery into nirvana in lieu of the slow, methodical, flower-sniffing method. And the new penalty for the ride on the magic bus?—head-on collisions with moments like these. Chidings from others have always been easily shrugged, but when one's own guilt-fighting resources regularly derail, Trouble has arrived. Freud called guilt "aggression against the self"; it's truly a masochistic ritual. And a novel experience, these formerly rare visitations of Sunday morning melancholy, when you lie alone as all seconds before your final breath, perchance womanless or even not, appreciating only life's empty, grievous soul.

It's a nasty feeling, especially considering the implication. I mean, some very disturbed clump of cells in the brain apparently recommends settling in a monogamous relationship with a good Christian girl, spitting out three kids and spending weekends staining the fucking fence before the ball game comes on. What else could explain such things? One sweats to fashion a unique life, a humble attempt to find his own joys instead of those manufactured and packaged for him; his reward is increasing bouts of remorse circling like a restless predator. And it seems to land and chow down on suckers over 22.

It could all be a subconscious preparation for the possibility of a very gross screw up, namely impending graduation. It's maybe the mind in a type of short-circuit, pathetically trying to lessen all shocks of suburban obscurity, just around the corner.

And the question isn't if, but when that inevitability will strike. Dwelling on it, life at 30 for an AOPer is a mythical, surreal concept. Whatever lies in store for any of us is a bizarre mystery. I rule little out—even a funny evolution into one of these street bums we ape just for kicks. Is it so farfetched?—not long ago these poor bastards also felt bursting with purpose, considering themselves enlightened rogues detached from ordinary society. 'Course now their individuality is suspect—or nonexistent—and they're reduced to a tired, vulgar stereotype, saddled with the indignity of indifference in their own and everybody's minds.

Or worse, what if some smug, ass-kissing businessman emerges from the AOP wreckage, with making big bucks the new challenge in life. One of those bastards with millions of toys and not a remote idea how to define true kicks. The only true kicks these fuckers deserve are a few in the ass.

At 20, nature is infinitely more redeeming after mushrooms, conversation clearly more interesting after a sixer and a post-coital joint with a just-met chick far more exciting than the same with a long-term girlfriend. But the image sours 10 years down the line, as the same face now widened, beer-bloated, tries vainly to seduce the indifferent 21 year old. Or at 40, with all the great mapped-out dreams of life in the shredder, attempting meager tributes to kicks and wild joys amid the great minefield of hyper-responsible peers, nagging wives and empty commitments. A fool road trip fraught with worries of flat tires and running out of gas.

It's become clear the thing that makes dreams real is being the age when they're still allowed to exist. Their culmination isn't necessary—it's their *potential* that's the redeeming aspect—that's what makes life fly. Name one bastard over 27 whose life is flying. It's no wonder everyone in music with talent bailed at that age.

And maybe AOP too has scripted a doomed journey, a Faustian exchange, for what in later life could rise to such a standard? The advantage people with rote, ordered lives have is the guarantee of consistency. Their relatively narrowed experience serves the great benefit of auto piloting them down a road less plagued with bumps and distractions.

Like a revelation on 'shrooms, those attuned to potential, truth and higher kicks are forever doomed to exist with such lofty ideals. I mean the stakes recently have risen to mammoth proportions, with each night out assuming a bizarre performance, an event to be topped. Constants no longer exist in any formulas—it's a snowball rolling down the mountain, expanding with kicks, idiocy, enlightenment, worry and doubt.

Wilt truly is no kin of his former self. Just a couple years back a subdued ex-high schooler—Christ now after 11 shots of Cuervo he's pledged a sworn duty to himself and any non-participators in life to *put on a show* my dear at a party—a human goofball vying for the attention of every girl, leaving not one with an unformed opinion of the madman. Or Tyce, who entered the university bearing polite, Midwestern roots, now somewhat of a local legend: I've met girls from Boulder, Greeley, Denver—four corners of the fuckin' state who've heard of the guy and would make him on reputation alone—he's surely had over 150 different woman—Christ, more than me and Wilt *combined*—and now is just a ghost to the formerly humble, self-deprecating sort with a sweet unawareness of what all the fuss was about.

The thing that made AOP work so well *was* this buffer of innocence, of naivete. Its nascent form was free from the baggage of expectation or historical influence. Now over the thunderous music of the party echo whispers of Tyce the Notorious, or acknowledgements of Wilt, the Clown Prince of Lunacy. With results already inured by a slew of expert opiners and judgers, it's obvious that just about everything in four short semesters has changed.

Thomas Mann wrote, "Certain attainments of the soul and the intellect are impossible without disease, without insanity, without spiritual crime, and the great invalids are crucified victims, sacrificed to humanity and its advancement, to the broadening of its feeling and knowledge—in short to its more *sublime* health." Maybe we've authored some lofty ideal of martyrdom, a foolishly inflated sense of purpose, finding it necessary knowing the whole thing's either gonna explode in our faces or fizzle in our fingertips more sooner than later. And instead of being on equal terms with the rest of society, we'll be victims of an ingrained, impossible standard: idle witnessers of an ex-life foundering in a sea of normalcy.

This whole AOP thing of late has acquired a self-consciousness, lost a purity of heart; it's been defined when it should have been left alone or trashed altogether. It's getting harder to keep thoughts of the grim future at bay, when the buzz of youth withers and nothing's left—when that which feeds the "power" runs its course. And with it, the stark realization that minus all the philosophizing and rationalizing, we really *were* just half-witted, stray mutts roaming the neighborhood, now caged and neutered. Maybe that's when the engineers of the world we'd smirk at, the Saturday night book-strokers without a moment of college kicks will slowly emerge from the dawn, like a revitalized posse, and will mercilessly beat me, Wilt and Tyce to a pulp with their TI 867 scientific calculators. As we lie there, three dying dogs, with blood filling our esophogi, we'll weakly gurgle, "But why?" And that's when they'll triumphantly hover over us, spitting out, "The cosign derivative of a logarithmic function is its inverse, you stupid bastards!"

38

So the last year at CSU glided by even faster than the first, and now it's just hours before my fourth year in college officially starts ticking away. The summer heat has already headed southbound, making way for the leafy, breezy fall days of northern Colorado, then yet another too-long winter. Twenty-two years old, and I'm a goddamned elder on this stupid campus. It's ironic—as we head toward old age and its accompanying insignificance, when we see fewer reasons to defend our grand individuality (for what??) or to espouse immoderate views (why for??); as we watch sideways in mirrors as the back crooks forward and drool flows liberally down a wrinkled crevice on the neck, this undeserving institution quite unfairly lives eternally, with its inhabitants forever youthful, radiant and vital. Eighty years can pass and these women will still have unlined faces, east/west breasts, sag-free asses and an endearing moral deficit. So that's precisely how long I'm planning to stay. It's a new goal, beginning today. I'll not leave quietly. Kicking and screaming the whole way, I expect to be a wrinkled bag o' bones escorted to the campus property line by security guards after one-too-many bouts of snoring in class and pissing down the leg. By then, having graduated into a cranky, stoop-sitting insomniac, I'll hopefully have found ulterior meanings in the world, like building the perfect fuckin' birdhouse.

But it's too early to be worrying about my 80th year at college. For now, my humble resolution for the upcoming semester shall be a reinstatement of the small hedonisms AOP was meant to promote. A return to the roots. I believe, with some fine-tuning, AOP can still resonate with life and joy.

Supporting that notion, Wilt just called. He rolled into town yesterday; we're booked for a full agenda of parties to hit starting tomorrow. So thus ends the book.

Tyce is gone—just up and graduated in the spring, the fool. He moved to Longmont, down near Boulder. The guy was always a poor planner—he passed too many courses, didn't change majors enough times. I haven't seen him since early summer, since way before my road trip. He came by the house on a Friday around 9 a.m., walking right through the front door and into the bedroom on me, my summer-sweetie Windy and our friend Patience, all semi-sleeping and sprawled in various directions across the waterbed. He paused for a moment and with a glint considered evening out the situation, then strangely wheeled and left with just a wave. He probably had meetings to attend, suits to press at the cleaners. I now realize there's a great disparity, a huge chasm between the college student and even the *recent* graduate—something radically changes even between great friends. I suppose if I ever I succumb to the reigns of graduation we'll be close again, and will spend the next 50 years talking about nothing but the half-memory madness that was college.

But I don't want to think about that for the moment. 'Cause tonight I'm going to grab a big-daddy jug of Canadian Mist, drain a third of it with Wilt and company and see what's what at Washington's. We're gonna make friends with the girls in front of the long line to get in, and bust through the door like the fall cavalry arriving. We'll get the DJ to play a decent song for once, and just before closing I'll find a sweet, honest lass to share it with. And the two of us'll sit propped against the vibrating wall by the dance floor, eye level to the flailing-leg craziness of the club, belting the song eyes-closedly like Jim Morrison—hell, I'm gonna *be* the next Morrison you fuckers just watch—and she'll describe her imperfect world to her imperfect friend, somehow in the perfect moment. We'll pool all happinesses we can scrounge between us, and squander every one like idiot gamblers. And we'll stave off sad good-byes by making the night a shade darker, and stretching it just a little past dawn. Her lips shall shine in the new light. Man this night, this *year* is going to be the greatest, maybe of my life.

Printed in the United Kingdom
by Lightning Source UK Ltd.
9598500001B